WORLD CLASS SALES & OPERATIONS PLANNING

A Guide to Successful Implementation and Robust Execution

Donald H. Sheldon, CFPIM, CIRM

THE EDUCATIONAL SOCIETY
FOR RESOURCE MANAGEMENT

Copyright ©2006 by Donald H. Sheldon

ISBN 1-932159-53-3

Printed and bound in the U.S.A. Printed on acid-free paper
10 9 8 7 6 5 4 3 2

Library of Congress Cataloging-in-Publication Data

Sheldon, Donald, 1962-
    World class sales and operations planning : a guide to successful implementa-
tion and robust execution / by Donald Sheldon
        p. cm.
    Includes index.
    ISBN-13: 978-1-932159-53-0 (hardcover : alk. paper)
    ISBN-10: 1-932159-53-3 (hardcover : alk. paper)
    1. Sales management. 2. Production planning. I. Title. II. Title: World class
sales and operations planning.
    HF5438.4.S49 2006
    658.4'01--dc22   2006010912

Phone: (954) 727-9333
Fax: (561) 892-0700
Web: www.jrosspub.com

As always, special love and thanks to
Anita, Erica, and Geoff for always supporting me.
Special thanks to God for our many blessings.

*"Don't worry about anything. Instead tell God about everything.
Ask and pray. Give thanks to Him."*

Philippians 4:6–7

TABLE OF CONTENTS

PREFACE

No more valuable planning process exists than the S&OP (sales and operations planning) process, or what some call SIOP (sales, inventory, and operations planning) or PSI (production, sales, and inventory). It was a treat to write this book, as I do so much work in the field on this topic and it has become a passion. S&OP is at the top end of the ERP business model. Class A performance in this area of planning delivers predictable profits, revenue, and capacity. That does not mean it is easy, only necessary and logical. In my career I have implemented several top-management planning processes that have developed executive S&OP advocates who, as they change companies and further their careers, duplicate the processes in subsequent companies. This has given me a lot of work all over the world and blessed me with many friends and numerous favorable experiences.

This book is a summary of details I have learned, some the hard way, about both implementing and maintaining a high-performance S&OP top-management planning process. Done correctly, this will be simple, will cost almost nothing, and will bring benefits every month for as long as you choose to maintain the process. S&OP processes are used in businesses from Shanghai to San Francisco and in products from ice cream cones to automobiles.

A few books have been written on the topic, but this one is meant to be unique in that it focuses strictly on the facts and details required to implement and maintain the S&OP process in your business and to get the most benefits from it. The first two chapters deal with why; the rest of the book explains how. Any management team that follows the steps in this book is sure to see great return. I wish you Godspeed on your S&OP implementation.

ABOUT THE AUTHOR

Donald H. Sheldon is president of the DH Sheldon & Associates LLC consulting firm in New York. He started his career at The Raymond Corporation, a world-class manufacturer of material handling equipment. He held the position of Director and General Manager of Raymond's Worldwide Aftermarket Services Division, which he left to accept the position of Vice President for Buker, Inc., of Chicago, a world-recognized leader in management education and consulting. While at Buker, Mr. Sheldon helped clients on every continent to achieve business excellence in numerous areas including sales and operations planning. After several years of traveling with Buker, Mr. Sheldon joined NCR Corporation, a client company, to work full-time with its manufacturing facilities throughout Asia, Northern Africa, Europe, and the Americas. As Vice President of Global Quality and Six Sigma Services, Mr. Sheldon was directly involved in the process improvement health worldwide at NCR. Then Mr. Sheldon, to limit travel, yet still support his passion for coaching businesses, launched DH Sheldon & Associates. He and his network of consultants continue to work with companies in North America to improve competitive advantage.

Mr. Sheldon is an accomplished author. He is author of the following highly regarded books: *Achieving Inventory Accuracy: A Guide to Sustainable Class A Excellence in 120 Days, Class A ERP Implementation: Integrating Lean and Six*

Sigma, and *World Class Master Scheduling: Best Practices and Lean Six Sigma Continuous Improvement* and is co-author of *The Road to Class A Manufacturing Resource Planning (MPR II).* His articles have been published in numerous magazines and journals, and he frequently speaks at colleges, international conventions, and seminars, including APICS (American Production and Inventory Control Society). He holds a master of arts degree in Business and Government Policies Studies and an undergraduate degree in Business and Economics, both from the State University of New York, Empire State College. He is certified by APICS as CFPIM (Certified Fellow in Production and Inventory Management) and as CIRM (Certified in Resource Management).

ACKNOWLEDGMENTS

S&OP (sales and operations planning), also called SIOP (sales, inventory, and operations planning) or even PSI (production, sales, and inventory), is a key process in many high-performance organizations. Companies that embrace it see high payback. This process has been developing for many years. It was probably first brought to the attention of the industrial world by Oliver Wight, a business consultant in the United States, back in the 1970s and 1980s. David Buker, another world-recognized consulting team at the time, was the messenger that brought this topic to my door initially. The year was 1988. Mike Stickler was the hired gun that made it happen in my company, The Raymond Corporation. I played the role of internal facilitator for the S&OP. As a component of the Class A ERP business model, S&OP offered obvious payback, even back in those early years. Much has evolved since then and the process pays back even more today.

I would like to thank J. Ross Publishing for the chance to write about my passion yet again. Through all of my books, Drew Gierman and the rest of the J. Ross Publishing staff have been great to work with, professional in every way, and extremely helpful on many fronts.

APICS has also been a great partner for years. I would like to thank the organization for many pleasant exposures. In my life I have had the experience of serving on the local chapter board, including as president; have been a member of the Southern Tier Chapter in Binghamton, New York, for more than 25 years; have taught certification courses; and have spoken at dozens of meetings and seminars, including the APICS International Conference. In return, this organization has given me many opportunities.

Web
Added
Value™

At J. Ross Publishing we are committed to providing today's professional with practical, hands-on tools that enhance the learning experience and give readers an opportunity to apply what they have learned. That is why we offer free ancillary materials available for download on this book and all participating Web Added Value™ publications. These online resources may include interactive versions of material that appears in the book or supplemental templates, worksheets, models, plans, case studies, proposals, spreadsheets and assessment tools, among other things. Whenever you see the WAV™ symbol in any of our publications it means bonus materials accompany the book and are available from the Web Added Value™ Download Resource Center at www.jrosspub.com.

Downloads for *World Class Sales & Operations Planning: A Guide to Successful Implementation and Robust Execution* include audit criteria for confirmation of S&OP process excellence and materials for training or course instruction. This material is available from the Web Added Value™ Download Resource Center at www.jrosspub.com.

UNDERSTANDING SALES AND OPERATIONS PLANNING

Sales and operations planning (S&OP) has been used in well-managed businesses for years. Also referred to as sales, inventory, and operations planning (SIOP) in many circles, this top-management planning process is the directional management system that sets the monthly cycle and calibrates the execution with the strategic plans of a business. The flexibility as well as effectiveness of this process is obvious. Businesses that enjoy benefits from this planning tool and methodology include manufacturing businesses, banking institutions, distribution companies, and even consulting companies. In fact, any business that manages demand and synchronizes resources such as capital, manpower, machinery, or brick and mortar to that demand has a need for a robust S&OP process.

The S&OP process is an effective, inexpensive improvement mechanism that more and more companies are starting to recognize for its benefits. Managers around the world are starting to focus on improvements in this important area of business control. The S&OP methodology is one of the hottest topics in business today. It is not a new process; in fact some might say that it is an old process. It is, however, garnering a lot of renewed interest— and for good reason: it pays off. Freudenberg-NOK, a well-respected auto manufacturing first-tier supplier known for its "lean" focus, is an example of this focus, as is Electrolux Home Products (Frigidaire), a market leader in kitchen appliances. Many organizations already honed their S&OP processes years ago, such as Honeywell and Nestlé.

WHAT IS THE S&OP PROCESS IN SIMPLE TERMS?

Stated in the simplest terms, the S&OP is a monthly planning cycle where plans for both customer expectations and internal operations are reviewed for accuracy, process accountability, lessons learned, and future risk management. Plans are monitored, updated at specific times, and reviewed predictably. Process owners are defined with clarity, top-management expectations and roles are clearly understood, and measurements are not only reviewed but are visible to the organization for communications and synchronization purposes.

As the monthly cycle progresses, process owners throughout the business are monitoring plans and updating the go-forward proposals. The forecast for demand is revised during the month, with demand reviews facilitating these discussions weekly. On the first week of the month, top managers are presented with options for approvals to forecasts and operations commitments. Inventory and backlog plans are either approved or revised by top management at this meeting.

In start-up, once the process is implemented in a business, normally it only takes about three complete monthly cycles before the returns start to become obvious. In some businesses it can even be shorter. The benefits are obvious and include improved communications and shared goals, decreased costs, decreased inventory, and increases in customer service. There is no magic to this planning process, just discipline administered in a top-management application, a discipline difficult to accomplish in many organizations without a formal process.

Virtually all high-performance organizations do some form of an S&OP process regularly. In these organizations, the S&OP is a monthly top-management planning meeting where metrics and performance are reviewed. Adjustments and analyses are done in preparation for this review based on recommendations developed from data collection. The key to success is preparation, data streams, and good data mining in advance of the decision process. Managing the data into workable product families is also a prerequisite for success. Historical data are always anticipated to be a major factor and can be. However, in reality, data collected from history are only a part of this data stream. New influences from the marketplace and actions from the sales and marketing team also must be plugged into the forecast. Data collection is followed by analysis and risk assessment. It is at this point that the forecasts influence operational commitments. Once these plans are all on the table, an analysis is done of the 12-month rolling horizon.

THE HISTORY OF S&OP

The history of S&OP probably started through lessons learned and process testing and experimentation in many companies. It is not perfectly clear, but probably some credit has to go to the late father of MRP (material requirements planning), Oliver Wight, back in the 1980s and maybe even as early as the late 1970s. Although by the time Oliver knew he had a winning formula, many businesses were starting to share experience through organizations like APICS (American Production and Inventory Control Society) and were evolving the process. A lot of water has gone over the dam since those early S&OP days. The first book to document the widely recognized process from the Oliver Wight organization was written by Richard Ling and Walt Goddard (*Orchestrating Success*, Wiley, 1988). About this same time, both the Oliver Wight and the David W. Buker organizations were selling video tools that helped organizations accomplish this top-management planning process. That's how long this process has been evolving. Of course, as expected, there have been many lessons learned and resulting improvements in the methodology since the 1980s.

Sales and operations planning has grown into a strategic weapon in a very competitive world. Companies of all sizes, from $1 million to $10 billion, find this process helps manage risks and gets everyone to the table in the handshake decisions, thereby resulting in better decisions overall.

To describe the process in just a few words, the S&OP process is top management's "knobs" on the business. If one of the top-management teams in an organization wants to turn up the marketing effort in some specific area, if they want to dial back inventory, or if they want to change direction totally and keep the entire organization in synchronization with any of these changes, the S&OP process is an important management system to ensure the decisions are implemented as top-management desires.

BALANCING THE NEEDS OF THE BUSINESS

Markets are changing every minute of every hour. High-performance organizations have skilled executives that understand this fact and either forecast these changes and allow preplanning or adjust to surprises by changing course quickly and nimbly. This is the case in almost every market today with successful companies. Once while I was working within the supply chain in the young-adult sneaker (also called tennis shoe) market, it became excruciatingly obvious that demand could shift almost at the speed of light as one sneaker style would go out of favor and be replaced by another just by some splashy new commercial on Friday night television. The problems that had to be dealt with were numerous. If demand grew rapidly for one particular style, the supply chain had to react just as quickly. Not reacting quickly enough could easily mean getting to market just as the next favorite sneaker was moving to the top spot in demand. This could only result in missed opportunity and inventory that would end up on the discount rack. Fashion, like many markets, tends to be fickle. Businesses that operate in these spaces need to minimize risk and keep both demand and supply sides of the business headed in the same direction, even when the direction is changing constantly and quickly. The more a market changes like this, the more a robust S&OP process can help minimize risk and manage the change throughout the entire business. No small task, and one that is very valuable indeed!

Slower markets can be just as difficult. Kitchen appliances, for example, are products that, except for electronic controls, really haven't changed that much over the years. Most consumers do not buy a refrigerator just to get the latest style. Refrigerators tend to have a reasonably long service life. This does

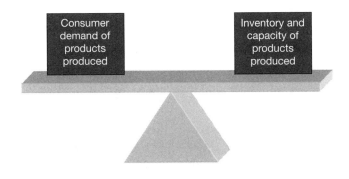

Figure 1.1 The balancing act between demand and supply.

not stop the need for robust planning. In this market the competitive pressures are enormous. When a business is making thousands of units a day, just a couple cents per unit can make a significant difference in the profitability of the business unit. The S&OP in the kitchen appliance market serves to help with demand changes as the market shifts. For example, economic factors such as an overnight oil price surge may decrease consumer spending or affect new housing construction start dates. Demand can move from side-by-side units back to top-mount refrigerators because of a shared frugal economic outlook. Consumers may go the other way for other reasons. They may unexpectedly begin to demand water-through-the-door features on cheaper models just because of the convenience. The S&OP process is the forced event that requires these issues to be looked at and decisions made by top management as to how the business will react to these changes—if at all. The S&OP does not take the place of good judgment or provide easy answers. The process simply forces the right people to talk about the right areas of focus in a timely manner. This often increases the chances of making the right decisions in the right time frames. It is all about supply and demand synchronization. (See Figure 1.1.) The better job that is done balancing these two elements of business, the more likely the business will succeed.

ERP AT THE CENTER OF S&OP

At the center of this S&OP need is the business system. In most manufacturing businesses today, the term "business system" refers to the ERP (enterprise resource planning) business systems. At the top end of this system is the strategic planning process that includes long-term strategy as well as shorter-term business imperatives. Intertwined with this strategy and tactical planning process is the market need, with supporting decisions on how to deal with the market variation. (See Figure 1.2.) Within the ERP model, the top-management processes must link with the operations planning and execution processes if the strategy is to be implemented effectively.

To clarify, when used in the context of this book, ERP is not referring to the software system, which is used to implement ERP. In this book, ERP system tools are just that: the tools that allow efficiency in an ERP process. The S&OP methodology makes up the top end of the ERP business model. The S&OP process allows the once-a-month approved plan to be communicated on an expected and regular basis. Management receives regular feedback from the organization and meets at the same time every month to assess the data and either approve or alter plans for the next 12 rolling months. There is no substitute for this type of regular and predictable (in terms of schedule) management direction. Organizations focused on lean manufacturing and/or Six Sigma are not immune to the need. These businesses are just as reliant on robust planning processes and top-end management direction. See Figure 1.3.

There are few arguments that support the absence of top-management planning. In one baking company with four major baking factories in the United States, the S&OP planning allowed the frequent shifting of product from one plant to another, saving thousands of dollars in freight in a market where moving product across the country added unnecessary cost to the product rapidly. In another example, a first-tier European auto-manufacturing supplier found that the S&OP process allowed much lower inventory to be engaged without affecting customer service negatively. Also, a plastics company has its S&OP process directly linked to its customers in a monthly sharing of top-management planning data. All of these companies share little in terms of market needs and customer requirements, but in every case, the S&OP process is a powerful part of their strategic competitive advantage.

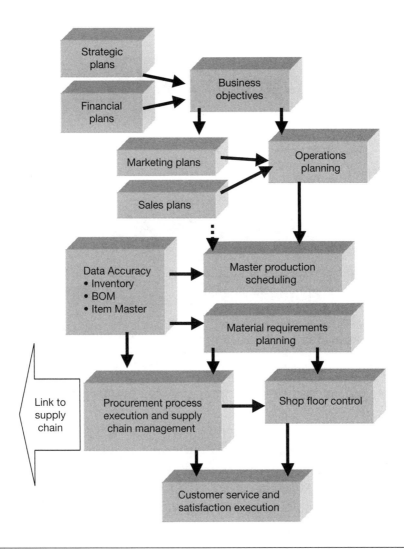

Figure 1.2 ERP business system model.

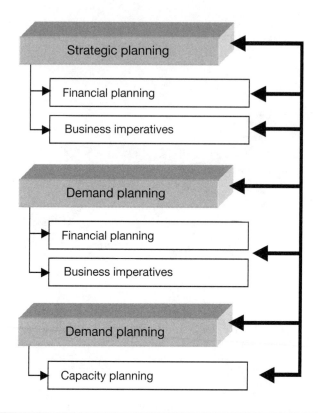

Figure 1.3 Top-management planning component of ERP.

SUMMARY OF THE ROLES OF PLAYERS IN THE S&OP

The S&OP process belongs to the top manager active in the business. Normally this is the president or CEO. In some companies the responsibility can be granted to a position slightly lower in the organization, like the COO, but it is rarely effective unless the COO is the power base within the organization or has the complete support and faith of the top manager. This may sound amazing, but the kinds of decisions made at the S&OP process can affect millions of dollars of resource, inventory, and most importantly, profit. The right people need to be plugged in and attuned to the S&OP cycle and the opportunities.

The S&OP roles will be documented in detail in a later chapter, but to provide better understanding, here are brief descriptions of some of the more important roles:

- President or chief executive officer (CEO)—The top manager in the business or organization is responsible for the following:
  - Reviewing plan spreadsheets in preparation for the S&OP
  - Discussing risks with key employees such as the master scheduler before the S&OP meeting to be as finely prepared as possible
  - Leading the S&OP monthly meeting by asking the tough questions
  - Keeping the meeting at the same time each month and insisting on attendance from key players
  - Acting as the process owner for the financial performance plan, called the business plan in the S&OP process
  - Understanding and evaluating root causes for process variation in the business plan accuracy and driving changes accordingly
- Vice president of sales and/or vice president of marketing—Depending on the organizational structure and size of company, the S&OP roles of the demand-side leader include:
  - Communicating frequently with the supply side of the organization
  - Attending the weekly demand reviews or at least sending valid authorized representation
  - Reviewing and approving the final demand plan (forecast) and updates to same
  - Distributing the demand plan to the supply side of the organization by the end of the month, every month
  - Measuring the demand plan accuracy and posting visibly for the organization to observe performance

- Serving as the process owner for the demand plan
- Understanding and evaluating root causes for process variation in the demand plan accuracy and driving changes accordingly
- Answering the demand-side questions in the S&OP meeting

- Vice president of operations—The top supply-side manager also has an important role in the S&OP process. The role includes:
  - Preparing the operations plan by product family for review at the S&OP meeting
  - Measuring the operations plan accuracy and posting same
  - Serving as the process owner for the operations plan
  - Understanding and evaluating root cause for process variation in the operations plan accuracy and driving change accordingly
  - Answering the supply-side questions in the S&OP meeting, especially as these questions apply to the build plan rate or capacity
  - Supporting the master scheduler in the full role of providing an accurate MPS (master production schedule)

- Chief financial officer (CFO)—The CFO is involved in the currency impact of plan accuracy. This top manager's role includes:
  - Preparing the financial plan accuracy by product family
  - Providing the measurement performance for the business plan
  - Reviewing root causes for any process variation within the business plan accuracy

- Master scheduler—The S&OP role for the "master of schedules" within operations is extremely important. The master scheduler is responsible for:
  - Leading the demand review sessions each week with the demand side of the organization

- Facilitating the pre-S&OP meeting at the end of the month in preparation for the S&OP

- Developing and documenting the schedule changes in the monthly operations plan

- Preparing the spreadsheets for the S&OP process (usually with the exception of the financial business plan performance, which is done by the CFO)

- Preparing the CEO with areas of plan accuracy risks prior to the S&OP meeting

- Communicating directly with the sales or demand-side team regarding capacity issues, lead time, inventory, customer service levels, and so on

- Serving as process owner for the weekly schedule accuracy (not normally reviewed at the S&OP)

There are others that can play a role in the S&OP, and these details will be covered more fully in Chapter 8, "Roles in the S&OP Process." Many of these people are support personnel that are involved in the detail work that makes both the S&OP and the company successful.

TIMETABLES FOR THE S&OP

In high-performance organizations the S&OP process is a top-management meeting that is scheduled at the same time each month. In many companies that schedule would be the second or possibly the third or fourth workday of the month. This schedule does not get preempted. People that need to attend put it on the calendar months in advance and schedule other required plans around this top-management priority. Having the right decision makers at the meeting every month helps keep the meeting not only effective but also efficient. It should be considered a "must" by all of the top staff.

A preparatory meeting is normally scheduled for the week prior to the S&OP and is attended by the master scheduler and demand people to make sure the risks are made visible and questions are anticipated and answers prepared. (See Figure 1.4.) The demand plan is at the center of this scrutiny, as

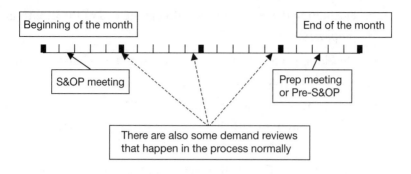

Figure 1.4 Timeline of the S&OP process.

this is the driver of decisions and activity. This is not to say the demand plan accuracy is the only decision to be reviewed. It is not. What is important is how much confidence the company's management team has in the demand plan and, accordingly, what investments the company is willing to make to support their confidence. There is no perfect forecast and probably never will be.

DECISIONS THAT MIGHT BE MADE AT THE S&OP

This book will outline the decisions and outputs expected from a robust S&OP process in detail, but at this point in our discussion, understanding the kinds of decisions that are made at this monthly meeting may be helpful. Here are a few examples of the types of determinations that might be routinely executed at this management system. Keep in mind that these are only examples and may not be the same exact decisions required at every business. The markets and resources will determine those specifics. These should be helpful, however, to get a general idea of the value of this powerful management system.

- Does management need to put more resources on a new product introduction to ensure schedule adherence?

- Is the increase in customer demand expressed in the demand plan appropriately supported by evidence and, accordingly, top-management confidence?

- Does the risk in the demand plan outweigh the costs of increasing capacity for the anticipated increase in orders?

- Is there enough capacity in the fourth quarter of the year?

- Will there need to be shift changes in the next 12 months for the manufacturing process?

- Is the marketing plan that was implemented earlier actually paying off in incremental demand as planned?

- Is the business effective in a new market recently entered into?

- Is there an adequate supply chain for the growing needs of the business in the near future and in the 12-month future requirements?

- What lessons were learned by the misses in demand forecasting in the last month?

- What was the root cause of the operations misses this month?

Of course, a number of other questions might be discussed at the S&OP meeting. The advantage of the forum is to have measures discussed, lessons learned, and decisions made regarding risks and opportunities. How does the management team, given the data required, continue to steer the business in the correct direction for success? This is worthy indeed of a regular process.

WHAT TYPES OF BUSINESSES REQUIRE AN S&OP PROCESS?

In my many years of helping companies achieve performance improvements through the implementation of an S&OP process, the types of products and organizations vary as much as manufacturing businesses can. Here are just a few of the types involved in my experience:

- First-tier automotive manufacturer/supplier

- Business-to-business packaging materials manufacturer

- Sporting goods manufacturing sold through distribution

- Molded consumer goods sold through stores like Target, KMart, and Wal-Mart

- Baked products sold through distribution

- Shampoo manufacturing sold to all type of markets

- Forklift truck manufacturing sold through distribution

- Kitchen appliance manufacturing sold to retail stores

- Business-to-business urethane film manufacturer

- Business-to-business engineering services company

- Furniture manufacturing sold through retail outlets

- Nail manufacturing sold in several market outlets

- Pharmaceuticals sold through normal health care provider channels

- Printing sold through numerous channels

- Consulting services (my business)

- Business-to-business aerospace manufacturing

- Radar detector manufacturing sold to retail outlets

The number of different businesses could be continued through several pages, but the diversity should be apparent. From baked goods and pharmaceuticals to automotive supply chain and engineering services, the S&OP process adds value. Businesses with varied stocking or inventory strategies (MTO—make to order, MTS—make to stock, ATO—assemble to order) are all equally impacted by the value-add of the S&OP process.

WHAT INVESTMENTS ARE NEEDED FOR THE IMPLEMENTATION OF AN S&OP PROCESS?

Top managers are always looking for good payback on programs that require little investment. The S&OP process provides this kind of payback. Nothing is required that most businesses do not already have in their grasp. The first ingredient is desire and understanding from management. This is done through education and internal marketing of the ideas behind a robust process. Sometimes when top managers talk to other top managers, the convincing is much more easily accomplished. Networking can be effective. APICS (American Production and Inventory Control Society) can become that network source.

WHAT TOOLS OR RESOURCES ARE NEEDED?

Implementation is covered in Chapter 12 in detail, but it is helpful to know at this point that little investment is required to get this process in place. The use of software is also sometimes a question, but the good news is that it is never—yes, never—a reason for slowed implementation. Today most companies have not used ERP systems to manage their S&OP processes simply because the software does not readily exist. There are various theories of why software developers and manufacturers have not embraced the process, but they are irrelevant because everyone has Excel software and it works just fine. There are many, many successful companies using Excel.

Oliver Wight, a consulting company started by one of the pioneers of the S&OP tool, has developed and offers a software specific to the process. In addition, some ERP systems such as SAP and a few others have S&OP process modules. Interestingly, however, the great majority of companies at this writing do not use special software. All that is needed is a spreadsheet and good problem-solving tools and skills. This is great news because, in many cases, it can take more time and money to implement purchased software than it will to develop your own simple tools. The time may be better spent developing the planning process rather than the software system.

Probably the most important elements for successful implementation are exactly what most would guess: management commitment, involvement, and support. Organizations without management buy-in need not read further because successful implementation is not only unlikely but next to impossible. This is true not only for the S&OP processes. The same is true for lean initiatives, Six Sigma implementations, continuous improvement processes, and just about any other improvement directive imaginable.

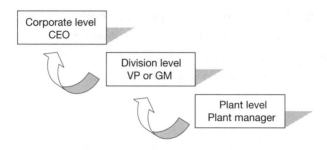

Figure 1.5 Levels of S&OP ownership.

Implementation is best completed by ensuring that the team members understand the objective and the vision. Well-done education and training, as with any project, improves the change velocity. This includes also having effective master scheduling, planning, and materials, as well as management of the materials. Without the full ability to put the information to good use, even a good S&OP process brings less benefit to the bottom line.

WHO DRIVES THE S&OP PROCESS?

The question of S&OP leadership is dealt with on several levels. The meeting leadership or process owner is easily determined. It is the CEO or president if done at the corporate level, the VP if done at the division level, or the plant manager if done at the plant level. More will be explained later if this sounds confusing. At this point, you need only remember that the highest-ranking manager in the facility where the S&OP process is exercised is the process owner for that level within the S&OP. (See Figure 1.5.)

A multilevel S&OP process is simply the application of the monthly management system at each level to make sure the detail supporting the corporate S&OP is as accurate and thought through as possible. In many small businesses there is only a corporate S&OP.

On another level is the question of process driver or initiator if the business currently does not have an S&OP process. This answer is not as consistent business to business. Some of the more common drivers/initiators of the process are the VP of operations, the materials manager, the master scheduler,

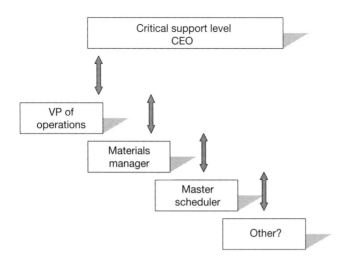

Figure 1.6 Who in the business normally drives the S&OP implementation?

or, the most effective, the CEO. Many successes have been driven from grass-roots passion supported by top-management vision and insightfulness. See Figure 1.6.

Many times those who take it upon themselves to lead this process, once the internal marketing is complete and the CEO is on board, end up positively impacting their career in a big way through the exposure and impact to the organization. I have known and worked with several such people and have many supporting examples.

This chapter should have whetted your appetite regarding the details behind a successful S&OP process. In Chapter 2 the full benefits are discussed, setting the stage for knowledge and a good understanding of the reasons for joining the many companies that have already implemented an S&OP process.

* * * *

2

WHY IS THE S&OP PROCESS IMPORTANT?

The question of value analysis of the S&OP process is one with many answers. There are so many positive things to say and describe about a well-managed S&OP process and the importance of it. This chapter is dedicated to the possibilities. There are probably others. These benefits are best divided into four categories (see also Figure 2.1): top-management efficiency, planning discipline, keeping the business objectives on track, and payback on investment. Details of each follow.

TOP-MANAGEMENT EFFICIENCY

In today's environment top managers in most businesses are pulled in several directions at once. The days we enjoyed in the 1970s when we frequently could play golf on Thursday afternoons, like my friend Tom Craver and I did, are now extremely rare in most businesses, with today's competitive pressures. Instead the norm is long hours and time spent with all aspects of the business, internal and external. Without the efficiencies of the S&OP process, either less of the business gets reviewed regularly or more of the day-to-day execution gets put on autopilot with little follow-up. This setup may sound desirable, but it depends heavily on a high skill level requirement within the ranks of

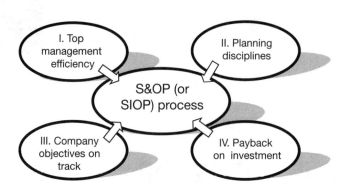

Figure 2.1 Top-level benefits from the S&OP process.

middle management. It also requires solid interpretation and knowledge of the corporate objectives and the tools available for implementation. Most agree that it is much better to have a regular direct link between the top steering committee of management and the rest of the business. The S&OP process creates the top-management adjustment knobs for the executive committee to adjust as they see fit. If the S&OP process is executed properly, there is actually linkage hooked to these knobs. See Figure 2.2.

The S&OP process has a regular predictable and repeatable meeting schedule, allowing for the high-level managers to plan and schedule their time. It also allows for very efficient use of their time, as the planning horizon in a robust S&OP process is documented in a consistent format with all high-risk "soft spots" visible and ready for proper questioning. There can be lots of different management reviews in the business, but the S&OP is the only one where all the manufacturing risks are identified and are, by design, made visible for scrutiny. Additionally, the process owners from all of the business functional areas are represented at the meeting. That includes sales, operations, marketing, engineering, finance, and, of course, the CEO. All of this adds up to a very efficient process for top management. No need to gather at surprise meetings, and no more grueling meetings where process owners waste time answering unexpected questions for which they are unprepared. In short, there is little wasted time and few surprises. This may sound impossi-

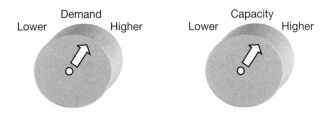

Figure 2.2 Manufacturing adjustment "knobs."

ble, but when the agenda is known 12 months in advance and the master scheduling department and demand management are trained in providing visibility to the risks, each month the process of risk management becomes much easier. That is not to say the decisions are easy. Business savvy is not replaced by the S&OP process—not at all. It still requires good management talent, as well as sound problem-solving and decision-making skills. The S&OP simply makes the process efficient by providing the opportunity to execute the required scrutiny quickly with, in most cases, questions being anticipated and answers prepared in advance of the review.

PLANNING DISCIPLINE

Discipline is lacking in many businesses, especially in those with less mature markets. If there is forgiveness in the marketplace, human nature seems to require it. I have always thought of it in a somewhat crude way: humans seem to do best where they are under pressure to do something or where they are rewarded for it. Planning discipline is the fiber in building a strong process of inventory control, schedule adherence, and customer service. Without this discipline, it is easy to miss shipments, be surprised by stock losses, and be predictably late on new equipment introductions. Discipline only predictably happens in the presence of accountability. Any other time it is a surprise.

The S&OP process by design forces greater visibility of the key issues or risks through measures and top management awareness that happens once a month in the form of the top-management review or S&OP. Even infrequent manufacturing process noise such as inventory shortages will be seen through the S&OP if it is affecting the overall capacity or cost of the operation. Supply chain management gets more than normal scrutiny in this environment. This all adds up to improvements in customer service and process performance, especially with regard to materials and inventory management.

KEEPING THE BUSINESS OBJECTIVES ON TRACK

It is not difficult to determine projects a company should do. However, the best businesses have prioritization processes to determine which of these objectives will really be done. High-performance organizations call these high-priority objectives "business imperatives," or in some cases, they are referred to as "hoshins" (from Hoshin Kanri, a management philosophy first used in Japan that is widely used in such organizations as Hewlett-Packard). No matter what these high-priority objectives are called, the result is the same in a robust S&OP review. Each month, the business planning process within the S&OP confirms the profitability as the marketing plans, new product introductions, new customer introductions, and incremental markets are developed, planned, and won. Granted, mistakes or bad decisions can happen in these planning areas even by the best management teams, but with close observation, responsive counteractions can be taken quickly. Many of a company's biggest risks can be attached to priority objectives and major changes driven for anticipated competitive advantage.

When the organization has clearly defined the top priorities or business imperatives, it is a natural process to integrate this improvement map into the tracking system, involving the risk management of the next 12 rolling months. That management system is, of course, the S&OP process. Each month, top management should be able to see the scheduled completion of these imperatives and the effect on the demand and/or the cost of going forward. If these priorities are worth doing, the schedules are worth watching.

PAYBACK ON INVESTMENT

What can be more important than return on investment, especially on large capital projects? The S&OP process not only tracks the implementation of large projects; it also forces visibility of the expected return. If, for example, a capacity investment in a new machine line was made and implemented, creating a 30 percent increase in output capability, the operations plan would show that increase in anticipated output. This increase would correspond with the latest project plans coming from the implementation team. The operations manager would be reminded frequently to review the status, for obvious reasons, but also to prepare for the anticipated questions at the S&OP review. Granted, this should not be the reason for preparation, but who can deny that as busy as top managers are sometimes, things can fall through the cracks? The S&OP review helps that not to happen. Monthly tracking would show the anticipated increases in production and the timing of same. Measurements close the feedback loop to communicate the effectiveness of these investments. There can be no hiding from the promises in this environment! Although the S&OP process does not guarantee successful investments, it does guarantee the visibility of the results of these investments.

TOP MANAGERS ALWAYS RETURN TO THE PROCESS

Most top managers today have career experiences in more than one company. Studies show that managers who have worked with S&OP processes in their past organizations are not willing to do without the advantage once they join new organizations. That has been good for consulting businesses that focus on implementation of the S&OP management system as part of a well-managed operation. It is difficult to maintain chaos once the window on process visibility has been opened.

S&OP processes, or what often is called SIOP (the "I" stands for inventory), are growing in popularity. Just ask Frank Wagner, vice president of operations and a top manager who has worked for three major companies in his career (all that referred to S&OP as SIOP) and avidly supports the process. "The SIOP process is one of the strategic priorities of good business management," says Mr. Wagner. "If it is not in place at a business, it should be one of the first implementations top-management teams implement." Mr. Wagner is not alone. Most top managers who have the privilege of working with a well-oiled S&OP process in their careers do not give it up lightly. Another friend, Westy Bowen, a Master Black Belt Six Sigma expert, worked with me at NCR and became an advocate of the planning process. He is presently implementing an SIOP (S&OP) process with his present employer in Georgia. Kevin Stay, president of Brennan Industries, Division of Mathews Inc., an archery equipment manufacturing firm, has implemented an S&OP process. This is Kevin's fourth implementation in his successful career. Tim Frank, CEO of Grafco PET Packaging Company, has lots of experience with S&OP in his family-owned business. He has been quoted as saying, "Why wouldn't anybody want to do this?!?" He now is attempting to implement S&OP process linkage to his company's larger customers to allow for lean processes resulting in less inventory and better service. There are literally hundreds, maybe thousands of these stories proving the allegiance to this old and well-regarded process.

WHY SPECIFICALLY DO TOP MANAGERS GO FOR IT?

It is no secret that top managers who understand the process and are worth their salt subscribe to the S&OP process. Here are some of the more obvious reasons that leaders support the S&OP:

1. It requires little time to execute.
2. The risks are made readily visible.
3. All the right decision makers are in the room at the same time.
4. It creates the knobs for the dashboard of their business.
5. It ensures there is linkage from these knobs to the factory.

See Figure 2.3.

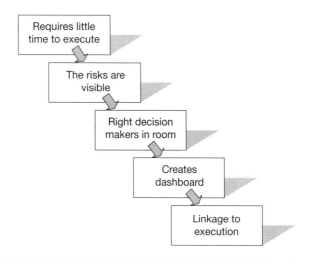

Figure 2.3 Top managers' "likes" list.

THE SHORT LIST OF BENEFITS

Following are some of the benefits that managers have experienced over the years after implementing a robust S&OP top-management review process in their businesses:

1. Significant improvements in communication between the demand and supply sides of the business.

2. Agreement on rules of engagement between the demand and supply sides of the business.

3. Less inventory and better customer service in MTS (make-to-stock) environments.

4. Shorter lead time generally considered high customer service in MTO (make-to-order) environments. This turns orders and inventory into cash sooner.

5. Smoothing of the operations plan for better capacity utilization.

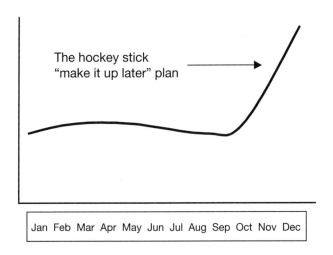

Figure 2.4 The hockey stick plan.

6. Handshakes develop in the top-management team (high-energy top managers with big egos need all the help they can get—not that many have big egos!).

7. Improved accountability on large projects and new product implementation.

8. More nimble reactions to required market changes.

9. Quicker identification of required changes in the future can minimize the "hockey stick" syndrome of always inaccurately planning a fourth-quarter recovery of profits or the "make it up later" syndrome (see Figure 2.4).

10. Improved profitability.

With all of these reasons, it is no wonder that the S&OP process has become so popular with manufacturing companies of all sizes.

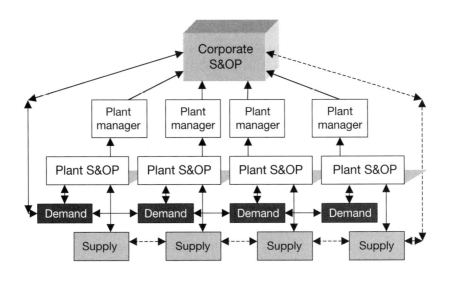

Figure 2.5 Multilevel S&OP process in larger companies.

BIG-COMPANY IMPACT

When thinking about the S&OP process, most people think of larger companies. It is true the S&OP process is most prevalent in larger companies because
the global experience within is normally greater and the challenge of keeping
all the balls in the air is much greater. Most any tool available is wise to engage.
In large companies the S&OP may be executed at several levels and participation may be through a broad base of players. If the business has multiple divisions managed as separate businesses, naturally the S&OP process would be
independently managed in each of these divisions.

In large multifactory businesses, the S&OP process is often done at more
than one level as commitment is gathered for specific plans and root cause for
variation is assessed. (See Figure 2.5.) The master schedulers at each factory
normally schedule their portion of the overall S&OP rate and the sum of the
plants rolls up into the whole. The S&OP review often happens at the plant
level with the plant manager asking the tough questions and then later at the
company level with each plant manager answering the questions from top
management. These types of reviews are frequently done on conference calls
with top management (plant managers remote and top management at cor-

porate). This can work quite effectively because of the scrutiny that happens at the local level in preparation for the monthly conference call. It needs to be said and will be detailed later in this text: The only way accountability happens is if there is the authority to say no during the rate agreement. It is not desirable to say no, of course, but if the capacity is not there, the S&OP becomes worthless if plants are forced to sign up for plans they know they will miss because of capacity issues. These problems need to be visible and solved, not whitewashed or swept under the rug.

In the larger companies most of the demand-side interaction happens at corporate. This makes it especially important to have realistic plans in place and for corporate to listen to the plants when they bring up capacity issues. Although not shown in the diagrams, the master scheduler plays a role generally by providing the data for review.

SMALL-COMPANY IMPACT

Smaller companies can manage the S&OP just as the basic simple recipe suggests—the two sides (demand and supply) meet, review, and agree on the revised plan each month. The master scheduler creates the spreadsheets with the demand manager, the CEO asks the tough questions, the CFO reviews the financials, and the VP of sales and/or marketing and the VP of operations answer the questions. A good time is had by all.

In many of these smaller companies, this meeting is the only time, short of the strategic planning process, where everyone is in the same room with the sole purpose of getting a handshake on plans going forward. In small companies it is not unusual for each top manager to wear more than one hat and therefore not have a lot of spare time. This makes the S&OP process extremely valuable for small companies. The S&OP process is appropriate in all companies, from $500,000 to $50 billion (and beyond) and probably could be applicable in even smaller companies even if all the hats were worn by one person. The meeting might go a lot faster, but the process is still valid and the agenda should be a review by the process owner. Figure 2.6 shows a typical S&OP attendee list in a small to midsized manufacturing business. Again, the master

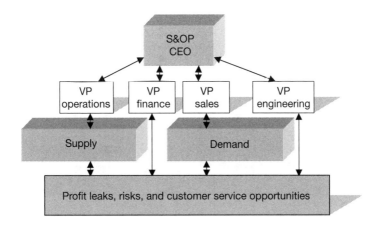

Figure 2.6   S&OP in single-facility businesses.

scheduler would typically capture and provide data for this important top-management review.

The benefits to small businesses are significant and not so dissimilar to large corporations. In small businesses, impacts from risks such as market shifts, new products hitting the market too late, machine capacity issues with long lead time to increase, supplier vulnerability, and other risk possibilities can be devastating—especially if the market has plenty of capacity elsewhere.

INVENTORY MANAGEMENT

Everybody knows that inventory is a major factor in both the financial health of a manufacturing company and high levels of service. The secret is simply to have the right stuff at the right time. Sounds simple enough, so why do so many companies have difficulty with the execution? The S&OP process can have a major impact on the management of inventory. Through understanding, documenting, and managing inventory strategies such as MTS, ATO, MTO, and ETO (engineer to order), organizations can begin to limit the amount of inventory and cash required to meet customer needs. This is all about handshakes, exactly and precisely what the S&OP process brings to the party. If these strategies are defined and agreed upon, the inventory levels can be calculated, thereby giving the financial model validity before it happens—

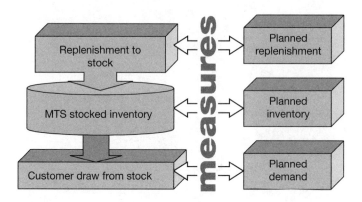

Figure 2.7 The S&OP monitoring of MTS inventory strategy.

which is clearly the best time to understand the effects of various policies. The S&OP has required prerequisites of product line strategies that will be covered in detail in Chapter 4, "Creating the Demand Plan," and Chapter 5 "Operations Planning for the S&OP Process."

Inventory takes resources out of a business and is a drain on healthy companies when there are too many people deciding what to stock. In high-performance companies with robust S&OP processes, the top-management team, not the planning department, determines what will be stocked. Sales or demand-side leadership is tasked with reviewing this strategy at least quarterly and in many companies monthly. Inventory is a good thing when you have a customer that wants to buy the items. Top management has the obligation to make the tough decisions regarding where the company's capital will be spent. Inventory can be a great drain on capital, especially if the turns are low or materials are purchased that do not move at all. Buying inventory is too easy a decision to leave to the planners alone.

In a robust S&OP process, inventory is a measured plan that is impacted significantly by inventory strategy. Replenishments are increases in MTS inventory, whereas MTO product families can be sold in great volumes without affecting risky inventory. Everything that is made is sold in an MTO product family. That is why it is so important for a business to completely understand its market needs and not make assumptions on large groups of product without looking at every part number in the family. Making these

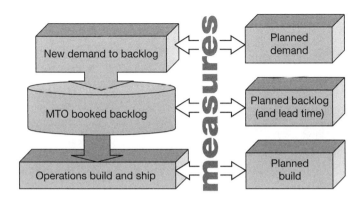

Figure 2.8 The S&OP monitoring of MTO backlog strategy.

generalizations is one of the fast tracks to obsolete and excessive inventory. To do this correctly, the demand side of the business must be engaged. They are the only ones that understand the customer need in enough detail to determine what the required lead time is for competitive advantage. Lead time is a critical data point and a major variable that is required to determine the inventory strategy, including understanding the customer lead time requirements and comparing them to the actual lead time. Any differences must be planned for. Either inventory or flexible capacity must be ready and in the wings.

Once the product family inventory strategies are determined, the S&OP review is the forum where accuracies to that plan are measured and monitored. This can reduce or possibly even eliminate the risks of obsolescence and excessive slow-moving inventory. See Figures 2.7 and 2.8.

Without the S&OP process in place and top management's involvement, the demand, operations, and inventory plans are difficult to monitor and measure with accountability.

✶ ✶ ✶ ✶

3

BUSINESS PLANNING BEHIND THE S&OP PROCESS

An S&OP process without direction is a flawed top-management planning process. The business planning structure, at the top of the ERP business model, establishes this direction in high-performance firms. The S&OP management system is essentially the infrastructure to help ensure proper process within the ERP business model—making sure top management's vision is executed. Strategic planning, while not part of the S&OP, is a major component of the business plan and a prerequisite to high-performance sales and operations planning.

The ERP business model begins with the top-management vision. In high-performance ERP, the business plan is made up of at least three components: (1) strategic planning, (2) financial planning, and (3) business goals. See Figure 3.1.

If business planning is taken out of the ERP business model and looked at by itself in detail, it can be viewed as a hierarchy of actions, only some of which are governed by the S&OP process. See Figure 3.2.

Figure 3.2 depicts the elements in robust business planning. High-performance ERP process does not dictate or prescribe methods for how to

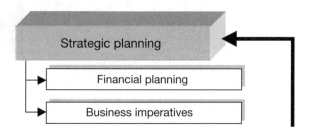

Figure 3.1 Top-management business planning.

determine the vision of market success, only how to execute these plans. In other words, if a company's vision does not meet any consumer's needs, even the best ERP efforts and process will not result in success. Class A ERP performance *does* ensure the delivery of the vision, however. For example, if a business's management expects high-quality sustainable experiences within the performance objectives they have chosen, it just makes good sense that the business has processes that can, on a repeated basis, deliver those results. This means it must be at least as easy to do the process with the expected goals in mind as not to.

There is a saying that is used almost every day somewhere in the world that goes, "Don't expect different results when you keep doing the same thing you did yesterday." There is a lot of truth to this philosophy. Too many businesses think improvement is about doing the same thing the same way but working much harder and faster at it. Nothing could be further from the truth. Achieving objectives requires designing process changes that result in improved performance toward these new goals. Sustainability means working smarter, not building a process that requires every aspect of the process to be flawless. That kind of perfection is not usually sustainable. It only works for a while. At best, employees get tired. Instead, an environment is required where people are challenged but can also have fun. Core processes designed to meet business goals must have that important characteristic. This initially gets outlined in the business planning component of ERP. The S&OP process within ERP will provide the maintenance and predictability through accountability.

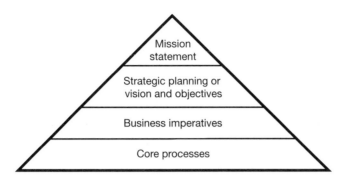

Figure 3.2 Business planning.

More than one manufacturing business I have visited has established goals yet not changed processes to make those objectives happen. Many times the objective is something like "increase sales revenue by 25 percent" in a specific product family or, sometimes, even the whole market. (That goal is especially popular.) This is a good and honorable goal, but there is more to achieving it than just writing the statement. Too many times among new clients, the conversation goes something like this:

Sheldon: Did you have a similar objective this year?

New client: Yes, we did. We had the same goal for this fiscal year.

Sheldon: And how did you do this year?

New client: Well, this year was crazy. We introduced a new product line and the market pricing kept going down because of too much capacity in the market.

Sheldon: Was any of this a surprise?

New client: Not really.

Sheldon: Then you probably weren't really all that surprised that you didn't make the stated 25 percent increase in revenue, were you?

New client: (quietly) I guess not.

Businesses often prefer stretch goals. In many applications this is what I refer to as World Federation Wrestling mentality—too often it's mostly for show. In the case of revenue increases, the answer is simpler than you might think. There are only two ways to grow revenue that I know of: (1) get old customers to buy more and (2) get new customers. Harley-Davidson gives us a good example that is easy to understand. New customers buy motorcycles. Old customers buy replacement motorcycles and Harley-Davidson-branded clothing, a major line for the company nowadays. Obviously, there are a multitude of actions a company can do to make either of those strategies happen, but the real key is in understanding and planning what those actions will be before you execute. Just after its 100th anniversary celebration, the experience Harley saw was a flattening of sales growth in motorcycles but a big increase in clothing. Knowing and understanding that strategy is key to growth is vitally important. Any tools to help with this are welcomed in most businesses.

The first step is asking the right questions. In the case of the new-client example, the questions that need answers are (1) What are the incremental products that existing customers are going to buy and why and/or (2) who are the new customers and why?

If a business answers the right questions concerning that set of objectives, it is forced into the thinking about the strategies of what additional products or services must be offered. Beyond that thinking, businesses need to understand how. For example, how is pricing affected? Does the business need to raise some prices and lower others? What new products need to be designed and introduced and at what timing? What is the competition going to do that will affect performance and strategy? All good questions!

These are all strategy expectations you have thought of from time to time. It is amazing how many businesses lack real follow-through processes for meeting their yearly goals and expectations. Strategic vision that changes predictable results almost always requires process change. One without the other becomes suspect immediately. The S&OP process provides a forum to review these process elements and to adjust monthly as necessary to achieve the desired results. It is not easy or foolproof, but if the entire top-management team is working together frequently to analyze the shortfalls of the process migration, the likelihood of success is much greater.

Strategic plans should be reviewed and updated at least once a year. Robust ERP performance and predictability suggests that this review happen at the same time every year. This makes the meeting predictable and process owners that are involved know exactly when this meeting is and can be best prepared for it. Normally this meeting takes about three to four days depending on the size of the company. Smaller companies can finish this exercise in one or two days. During the strategic planning meeting it is helpful to have each functional top manager give presentations on divisional accomplishments and expectations. This information can be helpful to thinking globally. Attendees of this meeting are normally the top staff reporting to the CEO or president, as well as a few key managers reporting to them. If the meeting gets too large in number, it can become inefficient. Probably 8 to 10 participants is the upper limit range for effectiveness. The danger is leaving some important input out of the equation. This can be remedied by having other key management or professionals present their input as a scheduled event on the agenda for an hour.

Additionally, there may be some value in bringing in an outsider to spur thought. Although this is not recommended in all cases, some clients have used facilitators effectively. At The Raymond Corporation, the company I grew up with professionally, the CEO would occasionally have an economist speak to the management team as the kickoff event for the strategic planning event. At The Raymond Corporation, in those days, it was a weeklong planning process that always happened in August. The deliverables from this planning session were a strategic plan governing the organization for the three- to five-year period and a short list of corporate business imperatives.

BUSINESS IMPERATIVES

Every business has objectives. When high-performance organizations establish their vision, they normally differentiate between strategic goals and imperatives. In many businesses I work with, there is a strategy to diversify into additional markets. In one midsized family-owned business I worked with, the president and VP of sales were brothers. These two were of the same cloth, aggressive and energetic and devoted to business growth. While this is

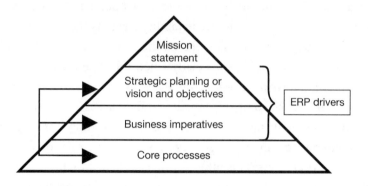

Figure 3.3 Business planning.

all good, the planning process was not as robust as it should have been. Unfortunately their aggressive approach led to a list of business imperatives about two pages long. This business never finished executing the list. There was also a prioritization issue in their business because all of the imperatives, by design, were of top importance. This led to questions in the organization about what was most important because there were not enough resources to do all of it.

Most would agree that all intelligent managers can think of helpful things to do. In fact, the real problem with bulk intelligence is that, often, *too many* things are dreamed up. Said a different way, lots of good people can name the 20 things a company needs to do for competitive advantage. The real leaders among us are the ones that can pick the 5 or 10 goals a company should and will *really* do. When resources are focused and goals are prioritized in this manner, more actually gets done at the end of the day. Business imperatives are these "must do" objectives in high-performance ERP. The business imperative list needs to be short. This is not easy to do. The linkage between the strategic and more tactical objectives, as well as the core processes designed to ensure these goals, is critical (see Figure 3.3). This communication only happens through predictable management systems that, not so coincidentally, are found commonly in a high-performance ERP process and more specifically within the S&OP process.

Business imperatives are those top-priority objectives chosen by top management to be accomplished in the next 12 months for the sake of competitive advantage. The list is normally the result of a top-management determination from a much longer list. When the list is finalized, management must be serious about the discipline to execute this prioritized list. That requires capital and resources to support the projects. If there is no management appetite for this, often the imperatives do not get completed, yet resources are expended without appropriate results. After all, if 10 projects are started but there is only time and resources to do 8, normally 8 don't get finished. The resources for 8 projects are spread over a larger base, which limits the completions.

From the viewpoint of the S&OP process, business imperatives are clearly within the scope of the monthly review. Helping companies to grow, this list of top priorities usually includes projects like new product introduction including introductions into new markets, relocation of manufacturing to low-cost regions, and price and cost projects. All of these affect the ability to meet goals and need to be assessed monthly at the SIOP process.

TOP-LEVEL MANAGEMENT SYSTEMS

Two important infrastructure events happen at least monthly and sometimes more frequently within high-performance businesses that require scrutiny on projects linked to the objectives. One is, of course, the S&OP process. The other is the project review process. Of a more global nature, these high-performance organizations conduct yearly strategic planning reviews to calibrate and adjust their vision, as described earlier in this chapter.

These habits of follow-through force organizations to see the strengths or weaknesses in plans even as the plans are being made. It's a similar thought process to "owning" something. Ownership makes you more cognizant of risks and potential gains. The ability to prioritize the objectives in a reasonable order is a powerful competitive advantage. There is no foolproof process of prioritization, only business savvy and intelligent leaders. One method that has proven to be helpful in many businesses is documented in *The Balanced Scorecard* (Kaplan and Norton, Harvard Business School Press, 1996).

BUILDING THE RIGHT BUSINESS PLAN

The Balanced Scorecard is one of the best and yet simple approaches to business planning that I have found and used. In their book, Kaplan and Norton suggest that managers look for opportunity and scrutinize four general focus areas:[1]

1. Financial
2. Internal Business Process
3. Learning and Growth
4. Customer

I like to add Supply Chain Management and Technology to the list, so now the modified list is as follows:

1. Financial
2. Internal Business Process
3. Learning and Growth
4. Customer
5. Supply Chain Management
6. Technology

If you take Kaplan and Norton's advice and also apply high-performance ERP management systems to this strategy development process, you will most certainly have a successful business planning model for your business.

FINANCIAL OBJECTIVES PLANNING

The financial planning model encompasses the ability to predict both revenue and profit. Few would argue that there is a need to have good financial forecasts, but many organizations do not practice the obvious. Family-owned

---

1. From *The Balanced Scorecard* by Robert S. Kaplan and David P. Norton (Cambridge, MA: Harvard Business School Press, 1996).

businesses seem to be the worst, but surprisingly, even some publicly held businesses still have very poor financial planning models in place. The excuses are always the same: "You don't understand our business; the environment is always changing and it is impossible to predict exact spending and revenue." Many of these businesses follow a plan that the finance people developed last October during the budget process. They then measure against this plan all year long. The accountants usually have their "divine vision" sometime around the 15th of October and come down from the mountain to communicate the requirements for profit and revenue to the rest of the organization, usually by Halloween. Within a couple volleys, a plan is agreed upon with little real process strategy linked to it. Frequently there is little linkage back to the strategic plan during this budget exercise.

Even more questionable are the "bottom-up" budgets that theoretically start from scratch each time. In many of these efforts, the result is the same: a budget that rolls up to a number that is acceptable to the stakeholders. The underlying assumptions of revenue growth at this time do not always get the scrutiny deserved. The result is a plan with little chance of accuracy. Accuracy of plans is dependent on processes developed that will logically and predictably result in the assumption list being accomplished.

The reason businesses exist is to meet customer needs and grow equity for the stakeholders. Financial information is essential to measure both equity/stakeholder value and customer need fulfillment. In a high-performance ERP environment, plans are always updated to the latest level of company knowledge. In the case of financial planning it is not terribly unusual to have two plans: (1) the original budget or operating plan submitted to the stakeholders prior to the fiscal calendar year start and then (2) an updated financial forecast that is updated at least monthly. The latter is the one that we will link to the S&OP process and post measurements against. Elements in the financial plan include the following:

- Sales in dollars or other monetary units by product family*
- Cost per facility and/or division*

---

* These plans are to be 12-month rolling plans linked to the sales and operations plans.

- Cost per product family*

- Inventory per product family*

- Gross margin by product family*

- EBT (earnings before taxes)*

Obviously, each of these could have sublevel drill-down plans to review at a more detailed level or to report to management when metric performance is not at acceptable levels. For example, a drill-down from the inventory-by-product-family report would normally include sorts such as obsolete inventory, excessive inventory, and days on hand. Since the main focus of this book is S&OP, the focus will stay at the top-management level of reporting and review. It just needs to be noted that there are lots of details in the preparation of good plans. All of the top-management plans are dependent on the other plans, including the three main plans: financial, demand, and operations. Financial objectives do not stand alone. These objectives cannot be made without full understanding of the sales and production plans, as well as new-product impact or promotions to market position and any capacity issues that might exist.

INTERNAL BUSINESS PROCESS

The objectives connected to the internal business processes are linked with what is often referred to as a "core process" or "core competency." In the business where I started out (material handling equipment at The Raymond Corporation), we knew that welding was a special skill we had nurtured and grown internally. As the business grew and we looked at the options of expansion or subcontract, welding always seemed to be a process we kept. The reason was simple. Raymond had some of the best welders within a very large radius (maybe the globe!). Many of our products were highly engineered for specific applications, and some were engineered to require hand setup and welding. Steel and associated welding still played an important role in the

---

* These plans are to be 12-month rolling plans linked to the sales and operations plans.

design of forklift equipment. All of these data aligned to say that we should probably continue to weld in-house, at least for the specialty equipment. I have not visited Raymond in a couple years, but I'm guessing they still do a lot of their welding there. It is a core competency—a process critical to their success and one at which they excel. A strategic objective in this type of environment could be "to develop the highest-quality welding process."

Also in the business planning space, another example of a possible business imperative could be "to reduce process variation in the specialties welding area to a FTQ (first-time quality) of 99 percent." This type of goal would include several areas—engineering design, process engineering, and welding operations, at a minimum. The difference between the strategic vision and a business imperative is the specificity, scope, and confidence. A rule that high-performance organizations follow in this regard is simple: Every objective named as a business imperative *will be completed as planned in the next 12 months*. This means that management must be not only on board with the ideas, but must also take responsibility to ensure that these imperatives are accomplished. These managers don't *do* the projects; they just ensure that the projects are successfully completed. This means supplying resources and capital, giving advice and counsel freely and frequently, and following up on agreements and promises—generally carrying water whenever necessary so that the objectives are met. Some managers are not willing to take that kind of responsibility. It can be risky. Business imperatives are to be announced as required project completions. Only the best project managers are to be empowered on these projects, and when support from engineering or maintenance is required, it is to be given.

You are probably getting the picture by now. If the team has a need for a process engineer and one is not available, the top-management sponsor will step in and get the needed support. If there is a lack of good problem-solving experience, top management must recognize it quickly and get the help or training required. "Business imperatives" are completed in the time frames in which they are scheduled—normally within 12 months from assignment.

Also, even though a business imperative may initially, at introduction, read like a single objective as it is listed in the business plan, in many more cases it is best implemented as a series of projects. It has been proven time and

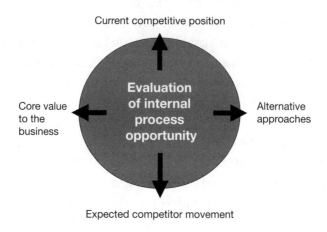

Figure 3.4 Evaluation of internal process opportunity.

again that if a 12-month objective can be broken into several 30- to 45-day projects, the overall productivity of the project team will be increased.

Internal business process covers a lot of territory and is normally ripe with opportunity in most manufacturing organizations. The right way to analyze opportunity is to list the core competencies and determine the competitive advantages that you already have and those that could be gained with some insight and resource. See Figure 3.4.

By asking the right questions and poking at all of the major processes in the business, high-performance organizations tend to create opportunity through creativity. These kinds of discussions spawn additional thinking—the kind that keeps you awake with excitement at 3 A.M.!

LEARNING AND GROWTH

Of all the topics, learning and growth opportunities are among the most important, yet they are often completely overlooked. Objectives in this area are frequently the most powerful. This plays to the leaders who believe that people are their most important asset. This is true in all businesses at one level or another. You've probably heard the old adage that the best managers surround themselves with people who possess better skills than they themselves have. I had a manager years ago that used to define good management effectiveness by a "delegation" yardstick. He used to say that strong, effective managers could be deceased in their office three days before anybody would find them. The philosophy is true. Sustainable high-performance companies are never made up of less-than-effective or unskilled people. The best companies attract and retain the best people. GE is famous for it. It spends a large component of its annual budget on education and training. As a result, many of GE's top managers have gone on to run other large companies successfully. It is no coincidence.

In the mid-1990s I was consulting with AlliedSignal (now Honeywell). The CEO at the time, Larry Bossidy (a protégé of Jack Welch at GE), measured managers in his organization by many topics he deemed important. One of those areas was hours of training and education. At the time, AlliedSignal had a 40-hour minimum requirement for each employee, and each manager had to report his or her department's performance to corporate. The training wasn't arbitrary; it was always linked to the objectives of the department and ultimately the company. Skills assessments helped in targeting the right training for employees. This helped their success.

In the late 1980s and early 1990s, the narrow-aisle forklift equipment maker The Raymond Corporation also held education as a priority as the company successfully transformed from a business with declining margins into a world leader. Ross Colquhoun was the CEO during this transformation. Ross held education and training as a high priority, and one really interesting fact I remember from these days is from Ross's monthly communications sessions. He would often brag that his department had the best ratio of employees to tuition aid use. His definition of "best" was the most tuition aid used. This was at the same time we were reorganizing and cutting costs in every area possible. It is arguable how much of the company transformation was due to this educational investment, but most who were involved at that time would probably easily agree that it had a positive impact. The payback is always there if the education and training are linked to business need. The exercise of using this topic to determine possible business imperatives is a very satisfying one when done right. It is an opportunity to invest in human capital and improve both the business and its members. See Figure 3.5.

Figure 3.5 Evaluation of learning and growth opportunities.

Looking at the skill set gap from a global viewpoint that takes into account anticipated market shifts and technology changes (both of which play a role in an organization's competitive advantage) makes the task of choosing the final list of prioritizing the business imperatives appropriately much easier. Brainstorm the possibilities using the topic focus from Figure 3.5. After scrutiny, compare the results with surviving ideas from the other category groups. Do not weight results in any particular topic until the final group of possibilities has been determined. Doing so will often create distractions from the original objective.

CUSTOMER INFLUENCES ON BUSINESS IMPERATIVE CHOICES

Let's face it, customers are the most important influence on business, probably even beyond the business stakeholders. They are a vital component in the prioritization of *any* resource assignment list. Customer behavior is difficult to accurately predict every time. That's why it is important to think about affecting customer behavior and not just trying to guess what customers are going to do. Even capital goods suppliers that sell to manufacturers and not directly to consumers are ultimately affected by consumer requirements.

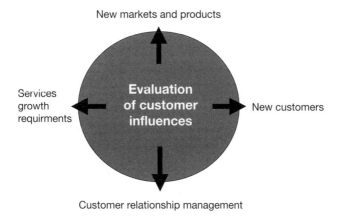

Figure 3.6 Evaluation of customer influences.

Fickle consumers (us) are never completely predictable even when a company makes an effort to change customers' behaviors. See Figure 3.6.

Since adding new customers is almost always a good thing, it may be one of the first areas to cover. Here are some interesting questions to ask:

1. What would our business have to change to attract 25 million new customers (or some reasonable number)?

2. What is it about our business that attracts our existing customers?

3. Why doesn't it attract the noncustomers?

4. Are these customers and potential customers different in some way?

All of these questions are the route to robust goal planning. This can even become easier if the vision is clear about where the business needs to go in terms of markets and products. Having this decisiveness tends to create parameters around the "new customer questions." This imperative driver often opens up fun and provocative discussions in the better-managed businesses.

SUPPLY CHAIN INFLUENCES ON BUSINESS IMPERATIVE CHOICES

In today's environment the topic of supply chains can be a frustrating one. There are so many choices that appear good on the surface but turn out to be bad once implemented. A lot of factors play into the final decisions. Many of these factors can create havoc overnight, such as the price of oil or transportation routes involved in disputes, fluctuation of monetary values, or more recently, terrorist threats in a particular region. Manufacturing organizations have little influence to stop or avoid any of these. Nonetheless, great decisions have been made that resulted in low-cost producers being established on the other side of the globe. While many of these decisions have worked well, others have not. Business savvy becomes a requirement. Little risk often adds up to little gain.

Keep in mind that none of these topic guides is the end-all. Instead, each is designed to get the right topics on the table and help with the process of determining the right business imperatives. As you can imagine, this same process would work to help with the vision development as well.

When it comes to critical-component suppliers, the process should be thought of as the lifeline, not the supply line. If you were going underwater in a diving suit that required someone to be on the surface checking air supply piped to you, wouldn't you want the best of the best? Your survival depends on it. It is disturbing when little thought is put behind the risk of moving critical components offshore. Building relationships or even partnerships can often allow an alternative and sometimes results in competitive advantage. See Figure 3.7.

TECHNOLOGY AFFECTING BUSINESS IMPERATIVE DECISIONS

In many markets it is not necessary to invent. Much of the time it is acceptable to innovate with existing technology. Automotive technology uses aerospace ideas and computer technology already utilized in other markets. Areas such as self-diagnostics and digital technology were well understood by the more technical industrial marketplaces before these ideas found their way into

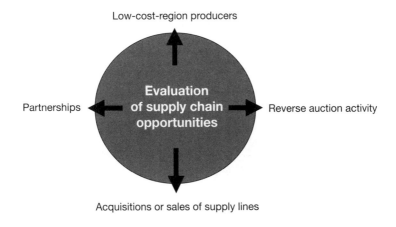

Figure 3.7 Supply chain opportunities.

consumer products. Some markets move very fast. Consumer electronics, for example, are not so fortunate with handoffs. They are usually left to innovate and invent for themselves. In just about every market today, technology is a major factor in determining the next steps your business needs to take for competitive advantage.

Once in a while I run into a market that breaks the rules. I worked in a nail factory a few years ago in the Midwest. It was interesting to see the technology used there in these fairly primitive products. The standard nail has not changed much in design since the square nail went round. Applications have, however, and that has greatly affected their market. Newer nail guns require nails to be sleeved to fit into magazines for easy application. Even the simplest markets are affected by changing technology. Getting the right priorities in design and capital spending makes a great deal of sense in high-performance business management. See Figure 3.8.

Asking questions in the technology space requires bringing creative people into the discussion. Engineers are often ahead of the curve (at least the best ones are). Every company has dreamers. These are the people that have an unending source for crazy ideas, and every once in a while, they hit on a really good one. A friend of mine in Wisconsin is like that. He has two to three ideas a day and at least one huge success yearly. I like to hang around him. He doesn't limit himself to ideas just in his market. He once designed a heat sink

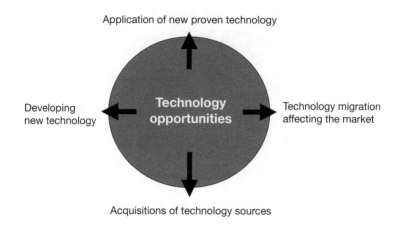

Figure 3.8 Technology opportunities in the business.

for laptop PC application and has patents on painting processes. It often takes many poor ideas to get one good one and, unfortunately, quite a few good ideas to get one huge market success. This puts technology high on the list for market advantage.

The topics discussed in this chapter, when analyzed properly, will get a team thinking about the right priorities and opportunities for the final short list of business imperatives. Once the list is developed, use a normal decision-making process to limit it to the right number matched to the appetite for capacity, capital, and management support.

HOW MANY BUSINESS IMPERATIVES ARE REQUIRED?

There is no perfect formula for the quantity when it comes to business imperatives. To discuss this, we can utilize another theory. Eliyahu Goldratt's book *Theory of Constraints* (North River Press, 1999) has been well recognized for years. In this theory it is recognized that if a business manages the orifice in the flow, or the smallest point of constraint in a process, the output could become more predictable. This process can be applicable in determining the correct number of business imperatives as well. Everyone understands that overscheduling a work center results in less process throughput. If a business overcommits project resources, it creates the same resulting problem. When adding to this the original objective design, the fact that the business imperatives must be completed in the next 12 months makes the capacity planning topic much more meaningful. The time frame requirement alone is perhaps the biggest influence in determining the correct number of top-priority goals. Management should empower no more imperatives than there is willingness to fund and assign resources to.

Imperatives become pretty obvious if they are linked to the S&OP process. The evidence of success is a common understanding of the list and a regular review of the risk points in the 12-month rolling forecast. Often, new product introductions or phaseouts are included in the impact of the business imperatives. These are almost always risk opportunities in a manufacturing business.

LINKING THE FINANCIAL PLANS WITH THE S&OP PROCESS

The essence of a high-performance ERP process is to define linkages within the business planning process. Through years of evolving the ERP process criteria, experience has determined that there is an optimum detail level for planning at the top-management level. This detail is referred to generically as "product family." If "product family" has a specific meaning in your business environment, don't get too hung up yet trying to apply your definition. "Product family" can mean different things in different businesses.

As you can see from Figure 3.9, there is an optimum level of detail for the product family designation. This needs to be experimented with. Trying to define a generic formula for pinpointing the correct configuration that would work at all manufacturing companies is difficult at best. It just isn't that simple. It is also common for a company to change the product families in the S&OP process several times before settling down to consistent groupings. The product families need to define the most detail with the highest level of anticipated accuracy. It is almost never part number detail. Incorporating inventory strategy (MTS, MTO, etc.) is often helpful. This means that there might be two product families for the same family or products, one for MTS and one for MTO.

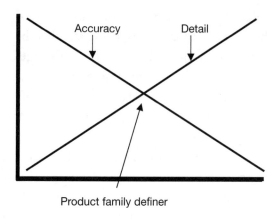

Figure 3.9 Accuracy versus detail comparison.

In some businesses there are more than two inventory strategies, fre-quently increasing the number of product families desirable for planning pur-poses. The S&OP must link to the MPS (master production schedule) process, and inventory strategy makes a big difference in the MPS. The discussion on the financials has to also start here, as it is critical that the groupings in the financial planning match the demand plans and the supply plans exactly. Picking the right family groupings and linkage to the financials is very helpful in maximizing the deliverables from the S&OP process. It is this insistence that allows the real power of the S&OP process to work.

PRODUCT PLANNING IN HIGH-PERFORMANCE ERP

Product planning is a key to successful market competitiveness and share growth. While this book is not intended to focus on product planning, there are a few specific areas worth including in your S&OP understanding. This importance will become much more obvious as the discussion moves to the next ERP business model process, demand planning. Good product planning in a business establishes market drivers and assumptions that the rest of the business can build processes around. This includes answers to the questions: What markets are we to serve? How are these markets defined? What market position do we expect to be in? Answers to these questions are especially important to businesses that want to cost-effectively produce products and capacity in anticipation of the demand. In many companies, anticipating demand is necessary due to lead time requirements of capital improvements. Too many times these requirements can be out of sync with customer lead times once demand has been introduced into the market. It is not unusual for business imperatives to develop from product family analysis. For example, in one food-service-related business, the strategic plan is to diversify into pharmaceuticals, a related product offering.

Timing may be critical for successful market impact. With the first product, product specifications are being developed and capacity is being procured. A business imperative may be to have the first production units shipped by a specific date. All the elements of business planning and the infrastructure of the S&OP process begin to play into the success or failure of the new initiative.

S&OP MEASUREMENTS FOR BUSINESS PLANNING

Some assumptions must be made as the business planning process, which is obviously quite complex, comes to the point of measuring results. One assumption is that profitability is a direct result of good business planning. This keeps the metric simple and also reminds everybody why the business really exists: to make money! The right S&OP performance threshold for this financial impact is 95 percent accuracy of the financial planning process. This would be measured in accuracy by product family—the same product families that will be used in both the demand plans and the operations plans. Keep in mind that 95 percent accuracy may not be as high as the CEO of your organization requires. We are only talking about a threshold of acceptability for robust S&OP criteria.

In most metrics within high-performance S&OP criteria, plan accuracy is the goal. This means that deviations from plan on the positive side of the equation are looked at as process variation, just as are deviations on the negative side. In good business planning, most organizations do not look at higher profitability than planned as normally bad. When a plan of $10 million

Actual profit results
—————————————— = % of accuracy *
Planned profit results

* If actual profit is higher than the plan,
the measure is automatically 100 percent.
No performance above 100 percent is allowable.

Figure 3.10 Business plan metric formula for profit centers.

Actual cost results
—————————————— = % of accuracy *
Planned budget

* If actual cost are lower than the plan,
the measure is automatically 100 percent.
No performance above 100 percent is allowable.

Figure 3.11 Business plan metric formula for cost centers.

results in an actual profit of $10.7 million, the measurement is still 100 percent with no performance penalty for beating plan. This will not be true with any of the other metrics. Also, if a business consistently misses plan, even on the favorable side, management must start to wonder about "sandbagging" in the planning process and may want to consider moving to absolutes as the performance criteria. See Figure 3.10 for the formula.

As discussed later in this book, in many organizations S&OP is applied in several facilities and not just the whole company. In many of these organizations, the facilities are not necessarily profit centers. In facilities where the financial obligations are treated as cost plans rather than profit plans, the metric is very similar. See Figure 3.11.

Be aware that, in either case, profit center or cost center, if the plans are sandbagged and the results are continuously beaten through higher profits or lower costs, the "better than plan measurement forgiveness" should be abandoned. If an organization beats its plan for three out of four months, it is most likely buffering its plan unnecessarily and should be penalized for it in the metric. In these cases the metric would go to an absolute percentage of deviation as with the other metrics in robust S&OP. When plans are continuously beat, it normally means there has been reasonably good execution, but just as likely is the presence of bad planning.

TALENT REVIEW

What could be possibly more important to any business than its people? In high-performance businesses today there is an acceptance that people are the most important resource. This is demonstrated by investing in the hiring of good people, in growing existing people's talent, and in helping nonperforming or subpar employees improve or get reassigned to duties more suited to their talent. To keep the movement in a positive direction, high-performance organizations evaluate talent each year to make sure there is an acknowledgment and documentation of where the best talent is in the business. Many refer to these as the "high pots," slang for "high-potential employees." Once a year each manager in the business rates the associates in his or her respective department for promotability, motivation, and special skills. Many organizations also use this exercise to perform succession planning. This entails developing a backup list of people who could easily or effectively replace existing key positions should the existing person leave or get promoted.

Having high-potential employees in your department is essential in creating a continuously improving environment. Normally it is these people who ask the tough questions and challenge status quo. Contrast this with "cash cow" employees, or longer-term process participants. Cash cow employees are highly knowledgeable resources that understand the existing process completely and often have many years of experience. This gives them an advantage of having seen numerous exceptions to the process happen over time. Good departments have a healthy mix of both cash cows and high pots. Without the evaluation, it is difficult to be cognizant of the opportunities in this area. Although not directly linked to the S&OP, ignoring talent management in any business planning discussion would be a mistake.

PROCESS OWNERSHIP OF THE BUSINESS PLAN

In the business planning space, there is no doubt about who the process owner is. In a multifacility S&OP environment where each facility is separately using

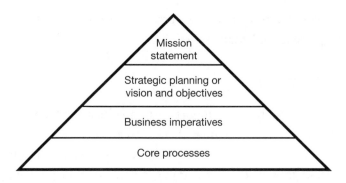

Figure 3.12 Business planning hierarchy.

the S&OP process, it is the top manager in each facility that owns business planning for that facility. In a plant it is normally the plant manager. In a division it is the general manager or vice president. In the corporate headquarters it is the CEO. The process owner of any process is expected to be accountable for, or "own," the process and the performance. If the minimum performance threshold is not being met, it is up to the process owner to either fix it or make sure it gets fixed. This includes reporting at required management system events, the S&OP process being one of them. In the case of the business plan, at a minimum, the management system events include the yearly strategic planning review, the yearly talent review, a monthly project review, and the monthly S&OP process.

SUMMARY OF HIGH-PERFORMANCE BUSINESS PLANNING IN PREPARATION FOR THE S&OP PROCESS

In a robust business plan, several process elements will be in place that establish both solid objectives and financial results. These main focus areas for high-performance ERP are shown in Figure 3.12. Once management has established the vision, the objective, obviously, is for the organization to get excited about making it happen. This is done through metrics and a management system. The right list normally includes the following:

- *Strategic planning process*—This event happens once a year and should be executed at the same time. The planning horizon covered in the plan is normally a three- to five-year horizon. It is generally acceptable that planning and forecasting beyond three years, given the current pace of marketplace change, would probably not yield much accuracy. Technology and customer habits change too drastically in three years.

- *Business imperatives*—The prioritization of top objectives for the next 12 months should be both defined and communicated. These imperatives naturally would link to the strategic plan. It is common for these imperatives to be communicated by top management to the rest of the organization at the beginning of each fiscal year.

- *Financial planning process (budget)*—This involves both a yearly budget and a monthly updated 12-month rolling plan by product family to support the S&OP process.

- *Financial plan accuracy metric*—This metric is posted monthly.

The business planning process sets the business up properly to execute. The next step in support of good S&OP is demand planning. Demand planning is often thought of as the mainstay of S&OP.

* * * *

4

CREATING THE DEMAND PLAN

The demand plan is probably the most talked about element of the S&OP process. In fact, probably no single process within the ERP business model, including the S&OP process itself, gets more attention than demand planning or "the forecast." People everywhere enjoy blaming the forecast for their planning woes. The facts support that, while easy to attract blame, the forecast itself is not usually the problem. The popularity of this source of blame comes from the frequently observed wide band of process variation introduced into almost every business by its customers. The truth—almost all customers are ill behaved. Businesses without unpredictable customers are an exception.

Believe it or not, in many businesses the demand plan or forecast is actually done by the operations people because the demand-side team members have not willingly acknowledged the required work behind the business planning process and are not knowledgeable enough to give forecasting a decent chance. In these businesses the demand-side team often only supplies an annual dollar amount for sales. This is not very useful, creating survival mode requirements in the operations team and forecasting efforts.

The S&OP process in a Class A, or high-performance, ERP environment creates a solid handshake between the demand process and the operations side of the business. This ERP handshake actually culminates in the S&OP process. Not only is this partnership attitude important for minimizing risk, but it also

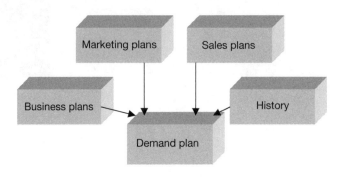

Figure 4.1 Demand plan inputs.

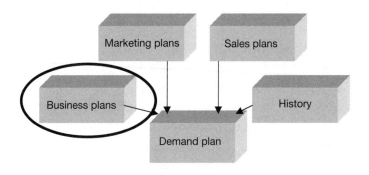

Figure 4.2 Class A ERP demand planning inputs.

creates an environment where everybody has shared goals and understands how variation from his or her part of the business affects other parts of the operation. This is, in effect, the essence of the S&OP process.

To understand the full process requirements of the building of a demand plan/forecast, it is helpful to recognize the inputs, shown in Figure 4.1.

The inputs are what make the quality of the demand plan. If the emphasis is on the right tasks and they are linked to the business plan properly, the results are very helpful to the business for making better decisions. For this to happen, there must be well-communicated, well-understood objectives with shared ownership in the outcomes, such as those discussed in Chapter 3.

Let's look at each input individually. (See Figure 4.2.)

BUSINESS PLANNING AS AN INPUT TO DEMAND PLANNING

Chapter 3 dealt with the outputs of business planning. The demand plan is where these outputs are put to work. In businesses that are continually developing competitive advantage, it is important to have the plans and actions tightly linked. Because management direction influences new product development and new markets and service offerings, it is extremely helpful if everyone is on the same page. The business plan inputs are probably the most important to the company's success. It is this input that directs specific resource assignment in marketing and sales and redirects goals. In high-performance businesses, it is not always about "following" the customers. It is about leading them whenever possible.

If, for example, management has prioritized a new service offering, then actions must be performed that affect this outcome. Metrics also need to be implemented to gauge if results are as predicted. A first-tier supplier within the food industry decided to focus on JIT (just-in-time) deliveries for competitive advantage with its best customers. The corporate business plan established the objective to build new small plants across the street from the company's best customers, but not until there was a partnership agreement from these customers. Longer-term agreements, in this case, mean fewer inventory requirements for the customer and shorter lead time. Shorter term, the business plan requires the sales force to sell the idea and obtain the signature. Without the business plan input, the sales plan may have been different. Such input can make a big difference in the forecast, especially several months out, as the S&OP process requires.

There are many more examples of business plan input requiring a shift in resource and effort, for instance, a new service offering to customers that currently buy only product, entering new markets, selling to Asia, and raising prices in a tight market for strategic purposes. Probably the next most important process input is the marketing plan. (See Figure 4.3.)

MARKETING PLANS AS AN INPUT TO DEMAND PLANNING

When operations people think about forecasts, they often think about *guessing* what customers are going to do in terms of product demand. It is common

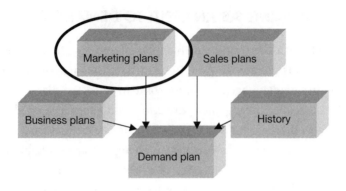

Figure 4.3 Class A ERP demand planning inputs.

to hear statements from operations people like, "Man, if we could just know ahead of time what customers were going to want, we could run very effectively and with very little inventory." This kind of thinking is only half right. In high-performance businesses, the correct thought process for demand planning is not to *guess* what customers are going to do, but instead *affect* what they are going to do. If you think about it, this strategy makes much more sense when linked to the business planning strategy. Most businesses today are not trying to repeat yesterday; they are trying to do things differently to continuously improve position in the marketplace. This means that the marketing department needs to estimate what impact each of its strategies will have on customer behavior. That requires commitment from the marketing team. In Class A or high-performance ERP environments, this concept is commonly referred to as process ownership.

An example is a company with a business plan that outlines two new products for design and introduction. In this theoretical example, one product is in a totally new market; the other is a new design for an existing market. Marketing will usually align with the new product introduction teams and assign employees to each product focus area. In many organizations the marketing department *leads* the projects through product management. If the new product that is also a new market for this company has three marketing ideas to implement, marketing needs to link its plan to some sort of expectation. As an old boss of mine used to say about *everything*, "There's always math behind it." The math needs to be exposed for a robust S&OP process.

Individual Forecasts by Topic

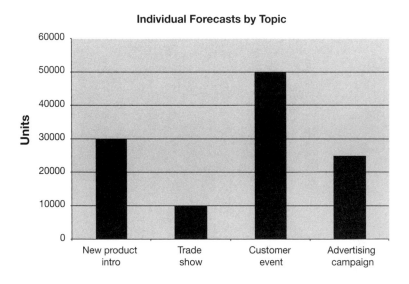

Figure 4.4 Forecast totals.

Let's say in our example that marketing's three ideas include one trade show, one customer event, and one advertising campaign. If the marketing group puts a value on each, some effect would be calculable on anticipated demand. If there was, say, an estimate of 30,000 units if marketing did nothing except introduce the new product through existing markets, market splash from the planned trade show might add another 10,000 units. The estimate is often best done if the potential new customers are listed with anticipated buy quantities. A customer event designed to create excitement for a few of the biggest potential customers for this product could add another 50,000 units. Lastly, an advertising campaign might have an effect of 25,000 incremental units. Doing the math, this marketing team could add 30,000 units (preexisting potential) plus 10,000 (trade show), plus 50,000 (customer event), plus 25,000 (advertising campaign) and get a total of 115,000. See Figure 4.4.

You might think that it would be a miracle if the 115,000 units was accurate, and you would probably be right. Though these forecast theories have some merit, marketing needs to estimate process variation just like the operations people must do for predictable success. As uncomfortable as this is to the operations people to hear, it needs to be said: It is also probably better to

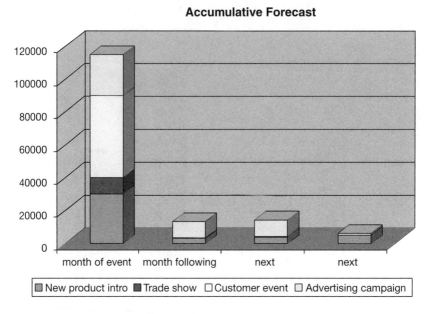

Figure 4.5 Accumulative forecast of incremental demand starting with the event.

be a little off on the low side than to have way too much inventory and nobody buying it. Marketing needs to factor the estimates. Add to this process owner-ship, and this demand plan process becomes quite powerful. See Figure 4.5.

The total cumulative forecast is unlikely to happen accurately without special circumstances and even a coincidence (like Mercury aligned with Jupiter). Even then it's iffy. Factoring for process variation just makes good sense. The factoring, of course, has some risks, and the marketing people need to know they will be measured on their accuracy. High-performance organi-zations should expect 85 to 90 percent accuracy overall in demand forecasting once accountability and ownership has been established. Don't forget that this accuracy is measured at the product family level, not the SKU (stock keeping unit) level. See Figure 4.6.

At the product family level, companies tend to enjoy the highest level of detail at the highest level of accuracy. This optimum level of detail takes some experimentation. If both the marketing and the operations people have the shared goal of accuracy in this metric, the job can actually be fun. Here are the

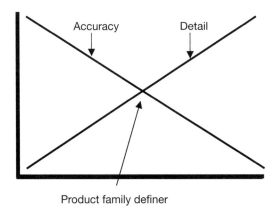

Figure 4.6 Accuracy versus detail comparison.

rules that work best. Perhaps writing them on the wall in the main conference room would be helpful. If organizations can get this agreement between the two groups, mountains can be moved.

1. The operations people need to stop pointing fingers at the marketing people for missing forecasts and, instead, help them succeed. Forecasting accuracy is much more difficult than accurately scheduling product manufacturing. (Operations people really dislike this rule!)

2. The marketing people need to step up to the plate and understand and acknowledge that the further the forecast is off, the more cost potential is generated for the company products. This affects margin in a major way. (Marketing and sales people aren't fond of this rule!)

SALES PLANNING AS A DEMAND PLANNING INPUT

The next input area to look at is the sales plan. (See Figure 4.7.) This plan is more calculable than the marketing plans. In many businesses experience also dictates sales closure rates and sales cycle times. In capital equipment, for

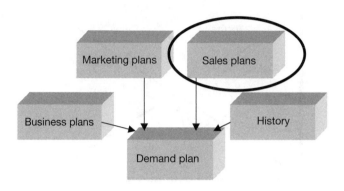

Figure 4.7 Class A ERP demand planning inputs.

example, there is normally a relatively long sales cycle, but it is known and can be reasonably predictable over a broad customer base. Other consumer products have very short sales cycles. In that case the customer reaction is relatively predictable. Sales are often linked to seasonality or some sort of market cyclicality. One clothing manufacturer I worked with that specialized in dance costumes had 80 percent of its sales in three weeks of the year (dance recitals are always in the May time frame). Another ice cream cone bakery client did the lion's share of its business in four months of the summer. (I found it interesting that in hot climates, ice cream cones still only sell briskly in the summer months.) Still another client, a kitchen appliance manufacturer, found its sales very seasonal as well. The most familiar saying I hear in businesses is, "You don't understand; our business is different." The truth is, there are more similarities than differences among most businesses.

In the 1980s at The Raymond Corporation we often missed plans. At one historical point in the early days of our "rebirth" and turnaround, led by our new (at the time) CEO, Ross Colquhoun, we started to actually calculate sales expectations, including the "math behind the numbers." During this exercise we discovered that our plan of increased sales and profit was probably not possible. With the number of people presently in the sales role and the projected closure rate, given the number of expected market opportunities, the math showed we would fall severely short of plan. The conclusion was that we did not have enough feet on the street. If we hadn't taken a statistical approach to this problem, we would have taken much longer to come to the correct

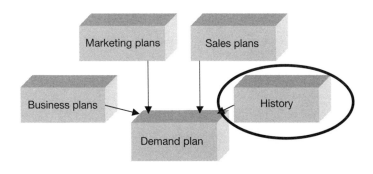

Figure 4.8 Class A ERP demand planning inputs.

conclusion. It might have even been too late. The story has a happy ending, however. The salespeople were added and Raymond became a market leader once again—and it still is today.

Performing the math behind the numbers in the sales function is critical. This can mean predictability in the number of customer calls, frequency of visits, follow-up on late orders, number of cold calls, and so on. Again, the business plan comes back to play. It is a major driver in the factors that could be appropriate in your business. The demand plan is the result of documenting and forecasting planned execution of the business objectives.

HISTORICAL INPUTS TO THE DEMAND PLANNING PROCESS

The last input to the demand planning process is the one that is most often thought of first, historical data. (See Figure 4.8.) The reason is most likely because, in many businesses, sadly, it has been the role of operations to do forecasting. The operations people know very little about what is happening in the marketplace, since they are not out in it. The only data they really have access to on their own is history. In many businesses, history projected forward is interestingly accurate. That is not always a good thing, however. Businesses that can accurately predict the future by using the past are often not changing the landscape in what for many are changing markets. This can often come back to haunt the organization in lost market share. This is not to

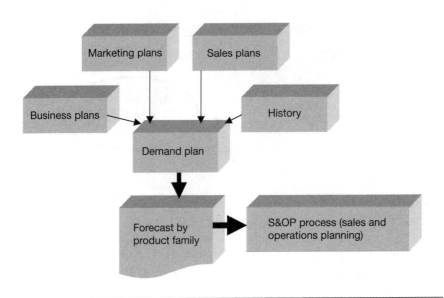

Figure 4.9 Class A ERP demand planning outputs.

say history isn't valuable—quite the contrary, it is. Within the data are the seasonal stories and the normal cyclicality that are so necessary to understand.

Today many of the ERP software packages are getting better at aiding the forecasting process using history. There are also other add-on software tools such as Demand Solutions and a myriad of others that can organize data and historical information to help statistically predict future events. These types of aids can also be helpful in organizing customer data and linking the data to the MPS. ERP add-on tools have come a long way in the last few years and should be considered if your ERP business system does not handle these activities proficiently.

Remember that history is the most difficult input to use accurately for demand planning in businesses that are making waves in their markets. In businesses that are shaking things up with new products and services, history becomes less likely to be accurate or as valuable. Historical data can also be manipulated in many ways. Software forecasting equations that allow weighting in any period you wish actually allow you to get whatever result you want. That is good and bad. Keeping history in perspective is helpful. Use it wisely!

UNDERSTANDING THE OUTPUTS OF DEMAND PLANNING

The demand planning process is done to help the business understand profit potential. (See Figure 4.9.) Indirectly it sets the stage for capacity, financing, and stakeholder confidence. The forecast is arguably one of the most if not *the* most valuable input to the risk management process of the business. At the S&OP process meeting, top management will evaluate the likelihood of the demand plan being accurately executed and accordingly will commit resources and cash. Demand planning is not a one-way communication or plan that gets thrown over the wall to manufacturing. Instead, it is a hand-shake agreement among all the parties. In essence, everyone tries to keep everyone else honest. This system of checks and balances helps with the risk management process.

The output of the demand plan is the forecast. It should be divided into product families and have a horizon of 12 rolling months. This is a major building block for the S&OP process. (See Table 4.1.)

The forecast is stated in product family terms and shows 12 rolling months of data. These data are used to determine inventory and backlog levels and to generate the supply-side operations plan. The forecast serves as an important and powerful communication tool between sales and operations.

THE WEEKLY DEMAND REVIEW

The demand plan is a moving/changing document simply because customers are generally ill behaved. Each week businesses are smarter than a week ago, and it is foolish to ignore that fact. For that reason, each Friday there should be a demand review held with all product managers, plant managers, and master scheduler(s). In most businesses, this allows changes in the current week to be quickly implemented and baked into the schedule changes for the upcoming week. In some businesses this may mean changes to the supplier signals (make-to-order or engineer-to-order); in others, changes to the manufacturing schedule (make-to-order or assemble-to-order); and in still others, changes to distribution (make-to-stock). It just depends on your business's inventory strategy—whether you keep inventory in finished goods, in components, or at the supplier's facility.

Table 4.1 Demand Plan Spreadsheet Example

Product Family	Jan*	Feb	Mar	Apr	May	Jun	Jul	Aug	Sep	Oct	Nov	Dec	Jan
Date 2 February, 20--, All numbers in thousands													
Line one	30	30	20	25	34	35	45	78	67	50	35	35	30
Actual	30												
Line two	30	27	22	21	20	25	15	20	19	16	15	12	10
Actual	29												
Line three existing	60	80	86	90	88	89	90	78	65	50	35	30	32
Line three new**	20	25	50	75	80	90							
Actual	66												
Line four	50	51	55	65	64	66	73	78	67	55	56	55	50
Actual	54												
Line five	5	8	6	7	7	7	8	9	10	9	7	6	6
Actual	5												

* The January column in this example has both planned and actual numbers from the month's performance; the balance of the months are planned quantities.

** New products are generally reviewed separately from existing products due to the high risk opportunity.

The demand review should happen at the same time each week with the same players. This way no one can say he or she didn't get the e-mail or notice of the meeting. A standard format should also be followed to ensure the right topics are discussed. Using Lotus Notes or Windows Outlook, schedule the meeting as ongoing and reoccurring so that it automatically shows up on everyone's calendar that should attend. The meeting can be in a central meeting room, or it can be on the phone. Conference calls are often the only option for larger companies where logistics are impossible or where it is too costly to meet in a common location.

In one roofing company where headquarters and the sales office are several states away from manufacturing, the weekly demand review is done with a videoconferencing setup each Friday. Management from the factory meets "face to face" via camera and television with management from the demand side hundreds of miles away each week. It works well and the addition of video allows improved communication, not always evident in phone-only remote conversations.

Agenda for the Weekly Demand Review Meeting

Following is a suggested agenda for the demand review meeting:

1. Review current week's accuracy of forecast for each product family.

2. Review upcoming week's forecast and any changes necessary.

3. Agree on any required adjustments to the production plan.

4. Determine any effect on the month's revenue or profit.

5. Review actions and agreements left from last week and new ones for this week.

The attendees are somewhat different from one business to another due to size and structure as well as job titles, but the general expectation requires process owners from the demand side of the business to be on call or at the meeting.

Attendees of the Weekly Demand Review Meeting

The following list is a typical list of attendees:

1. Product managers (demand side)

2. Plant managers (supply side)

3. Operations VP (supply side)

4. Master schedulers (supply side)

5. Optional attendees:
   a. Sales VP (demand side)
   b. Marketing VP (demand side)

In some larger organizations people come in and out of the meeting according to prescheduled time slots for specific product families. For exam-

Sample month — January, where the first day of the month happens to be a Monday

	Mon	Tue	Wed	Thu	Fri
Week 1		S&OP			Demand review
Week 2					Demand review
Week 3					Demand review
Week 4					Pre-S&OP review

Figure 4.10 Monthly demand review schedule.

ple, the product manager for Line 2 does not need to be on the call when Line 1 is being discussed unless it is of some specific interest due to shared resources, and so on. If multiplants are involved, usually master schedulers at each facility are only interested in lines that affect their facility and schedule. This discussion is not to keep people out of the meeting for any other reason than to minimize their time commitment. Anybody who wishes to and has time is welcome. In some very large organizations, the infrastructure is deep enough that it is not necessary for VP-level personnel to attend. (The "too many levels in an organization" discussion will be left for another day—or, in this case, book.) The weekly demand review meeting is a great communication tool between the demand and operations sides of the business and a prerequisite to optimal S&OP performance.

When someone is unable attend the demand review due to illness, vacation, or customer requirements, a replacement is to be named and to attend with full decision-making authority in the person's absence. Once a month, usually the last demand review meeting of the month, the agenda changes in preparation for the soon-to-occur S&OP process review. This last demand review of the month is for the purpose of sharing the monthly results as well as to see all deviations from the original monthly plan, as it was locked for review at the beginning of the month. The Oliver Wight consulting organization's methodology often refers to this meeting simply as the "pre-S&OP" process. Because of the late Oliver Wight's influence in this space, it is appropriate to call it that. Regardless of what you call this meeting, however, the weekly demand review prior to the S&OP needs to have a monthly emphasis that is not necessarily part of the normal weekly meeting. See Figure 4.10 for the monthly S&OP process schedule layout.

The agenda for the pre-S&OP meeting is not so unlike the weekly demand review. The biggest difference is twofold:

1. The discussion regarding demand and production plan variation is more of a summary for the month rather than just the last week's variation.

2. There is a full acknowledgment that the S&OP meeting is only a few days away and questions need to have both answers and proposals for improvement. This acknowledgment makes the meeting more productive because attendees know that there is a deadline pending. With everybody in the room to make important decisions, the process can be quite efficient.

PROCESS OWNERSHIP IN THE DEMAND PLAN

The process ownership in demand planning can also differ from business to business because of variation in organization structure and job titles. At The Raymond Corporation, the VP of marketing had all the product managers reporting to her. Product managers had a huge influence on the business and were aligned by product family—the same product families used in the S&OP process and demand planning. Product managers determined marketing plans and helped manage the sales force policy at the distributors, which, in this case, were independent dealerships. The product managers were responsible for gathering information from the dealers and massaging it to their liking, and for delivering forecasts to the VP of marketing. She would in turn review them and revise when necessary and then deliver these estimates to the S&OP process, where the records would be reviewed, revised (again) if needed, and blessed by the complete top management team. The VP of marketing was ultimately the process owner for demand planning—although she got lots of help from the VP of sales and both were obviously present for the demand accuracy review during both the end-of-month demand review (pre-S&OP) and the S&OP.

In other smaller businesses the VP of sales can be also responsible for marketing. In these businesses everybody from the demand side of the business reports to the VP of sales. There is little question who is the process owner in these organizations—the VP of sales. One approach to avoid if possible is to have the process ownership for demand planning accuracy delegated too far down the organization. It is the president or CEO's job to ask the tough questions. The vice-president level is normally the appropriate level for process ownership to reside for the demand plan accuracy, and this high-level VP should answer to that accountability. It takes a lot of help from the organization to get it right, and the more handshakes there are and, as in most processes, the more work put into the preparation, the more likely that there will be a successful S&OP process.

In these smaller organizations it is not unusual for a demand planner position to exist. The demand planner normally is the center of data collection for the demand side of the business. This person collects information from the field, account managers, customers as appropriate, and demand-side top management. Once this information is gathered and sorted by product family, it is presented to the demand plan process owner (VP of sales and marketing) for adjustment and approval. The demand planner also can be a big aid to the master scheduler when sorting through schedule changes due to conflicts that develop through the course of normal business. The demand manager is not normally the process owner. Process ownership remains with the top manager from the demand-side process.

Process ownership means that the "buck stops here." Accuracy is the goal, and the process owner is responsible for providing evidence of both learning and actions to improve the existing demand accuracy by product family. Process ownership is a role played out at several management system events throughout the month in high-performance organizations. The S&OP meeting is just one of them.

Table 4.2 Demand Plan Accuracy Calculation

	Accuracy
Product Family 1	100
Product Family 2	97
Product Family 3	90
Product Family 4	92
Product Family 5	100
Total performance	= (100 + 97 + 90 + 92 + 100) / 5 families or 95.8%

THE MEASUREMENT PROCESS FOR DEMAND PLAN ACCURACY

The measurement process for demand planning accuracy is simple. The calculation is always from the product-family-level data and normally has an acceptability threshold of 90 percent. The measurement is posted as the average accuracy by product family. Some people get a little uncomfortable with average accuracy because accuracy itself is depicted as an average. Table 4.2 shows how demand accuracy is calculated for the S&OP process review.

The data are from the January performance shown in Table 4.1. The overall accuracy is calculated from the accuracy of each family. The family performance numbers in January from Table 4.1 would calculate per the following example in Table 4.2. See also Table 4.3.

BLANKET ORDERS AS THEY APPLY TO THE MEASUREMENT

The measurement standards are proven metrics from the Class A ERP certification process, a performance goal that many companies have adopted over the years with great success. One of the early questions about measurement in the demand planning space is in regard to interpretation of the measurement rules. The forecast and the actual are not always what they seem. For example, most companies have blanket order agreements with their best customers. This just makes good sense. It eliminates unnecessary documentation and paperwork flow. Many companies make the mistake of using the blanket order as the "actual order" in the demand planning metric. This often *does not* make

Table 4.3 Demand Plan Spreadsheet Example

Product Family	Jan*	Feb	Mar	Apr	May	Jun	Jul	Aug	Sep	Oct	Nov	Dec	Jan
	Date 2 February, 20--, All numbers in thousands												
Line one	30	30	20	25	34	35	45	78	67	50	35	35	30
Actual	30												
Performance	100%												
Line two	30	27	22	21	20	25	15	20	19	16	15	12	10
Actual	29												
Performance	97%												
Line three existing	60	80	86	90	88	89	90	78	65	50	35	30	32
Line three new**	20	25	50	75	80	90							
Actual	66												
Performance	90%												
Line four	50	51	55	65	64	66	73	78	67	55	56	55	50
Actual	54												
Performance	92%												
Line five	5	8	6	7	7	7	8	9	10	9	7	6	6
Actual	5												
Performance	100%												
Perf. Total	95.8%												

* The January column in this example has both planned and actual numbers from the month's performance; the balance of the months are planned quantities.
** New products are generally reviewed separately from existing products due to the high risk opportunity.

sense because the customers normally give a blanket order and then change the quantities or schedule just prior to the ship date. Most of the time, blanket orders are *just forecasts*. No argument—these signals are pretty firm. Most supply chain agreements include purchasing obligations for products in blanket orders up to certain limits. Nonetheless these signals are really not much more than a heads-up that the customer is about to schedule something. Good suppliers are ready with some level of anticipated inventory or capacity.

The metric is designed to measure accuracy of the forecast. Unless you have a special understanding with your customers and their blanket orders are firm, it is recommended that blanket orders are acknowledged as forecasts only. The real order is the firmed-up schedule a week or so out even if there are no changes to the blanket forecast. No change simply means 100 percent accuracy for that segment of the forecast.

One automotive supplier in Europe, Volkswagen, would give a blanket production order (PO) out several weeks to its top-tier suppliers. Each week the releases from the blanket were updated to the supplier. The sales organization in the supplier company was responsible for forecasting how many firm released units per product family the manufacturer would get firm-scheduled by Volkswagen for the month, regardless of the blanket order quantities received. In this case the supplier sold to several automobile manufacturers, and when it added the total outlook from all auto-building customers, the result was much higher than the overall auto-build expectation. This meant the blanket forecasts, at least in some cases, had to be adjusted if accuracy were to even stand a chance of happening. Massaging the customer's information is almost always necessary. The closer you get to the end-item consumer in the food chain, the more applicable this rule seems to be. The reason is simple: unruly customers.

Demand planning is a monthly metric. The demand plan, as a living document, is updated as required throughout the month, obviously, but for measurement purposes only, the "plan of record" remains locked. This lock happens at the S&OP meeting each month and is measured for monthly accuracy and posted. Reporting is only normally done in percentage format at the end-of-month demand review and the S&OP meeting. The focus should not be only on accuracy but also on what can be learned from the inaccuracies experienced. Demand planning in a high-performance organization is about shared goals, process ownership clearly defined, and a management system made up of the S&OP and the weekly demand review. This keeps everyone communicating properly.

The next major process in the ERP business model is the operations plan. The manufacturing issues in this supply-side planning process are discussed in more detail in Chapter 5. As defined in Figure 4.11, the operations plan is a

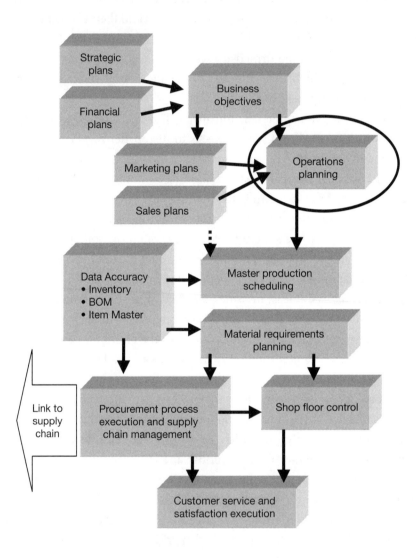

Figure 4.11 ERP business system model.

main process with many important inputs and outputs. This next process is the other side of the necessary handshake for the prerequisite, demand planning.

* * * *

5

OPERATIONS PLANNING FOR THE S&OP PROCESS

It is not a difficult guess that most people who read this book are probably operations people by trade. Materials planning and scheduling are included in this operations category. Many of you have been in production or production planning most of your life. Operations people have the sights, sounds, and smells of the factory in their blood. Making things from raw materials and doing it with speed and flexibility is an art well appreciated by these folks. That is what operations planning is all about, planning and executing plans to manufacture goods with cost-effectiveness, speed, and high customer satisfaction. Robust ERP process definitions in the operations planning space help to ensure predictable outcomes to schedules. Like so many topics in this book, operations planning is very supportive of a high-performance S&OP process. By now it should be obvious that this top-management planning process requires many people to work toward one goal, each carrying his or her own weight and delivering results. Many hands make many handshakes!

INVENTORY STRATEGY

Operations planning starts with a demand plan input along with an understanding of the capacities and process expectations of the business. With this understanding comes a necessary definition of inventory strategy. This important process design is too often not given the credit it deserves. Inventory strategy is a key modeling element in the ERP business model. Inventory strategy used in this context is the positioning of inventory in the overall manufacturing, supply chain, and customer service processes.

In the business where I cut my professional teeth, we had a product mix of 80 percent MTO or ETO and 20 percent MTS. Understanding and acknowledging the realities accurately helps a company put the right process in place to meet inventory goals and cost requirements. Many businesses, especially at the top-management level, think they know their company's inventory stocking strategy, but in actuality, these managers are not close enough to the process to see that it is different than their perception. These misunderstandings can lead to unnecessary costs. It usually is in the form of MTS perceived as MTO. Not possible this confusion could exist, you think? It is very possible. In fact, more than half the businesses I go into have serious deficiencies in their understanding of their organization's inventory stocking strategy. Most of this comes from believing that because they do not build anything they do not have an order for, they cannot stock. Many of these customers change the schedules at the last minute and their suppliers have stock on hand to anticipate this schedule rearrangement. This is MTS strategy and should be acknowledged as such.

In an MTO business, the inventory is usually planned at a raw material level, and the process of machining, welding, subassembling, and assembling the materials does not happen until the customer enters the order with the required specifications. Lots of companies use an MTO strategy. Many more are moving from MTS to MTO to save manufacturing costs and even to improve service.

A company that has received a lot of attention around its inventory strategy is Dell Computer. Its inventory strategy is to master schedule the subassemblies and complete the final assembly at the last moment when the customer signal is received. This allows the company to provide configuration flexibility specific to a customer's need and yet allows fast cycle time, from customer signal to shipment. Dell's inventory strategy is known as ATO (assemble to order). Figure 5.1 gives a sense of how these strategies fit together. Keep in mind that most companies do not use just one of the strategies. It is not

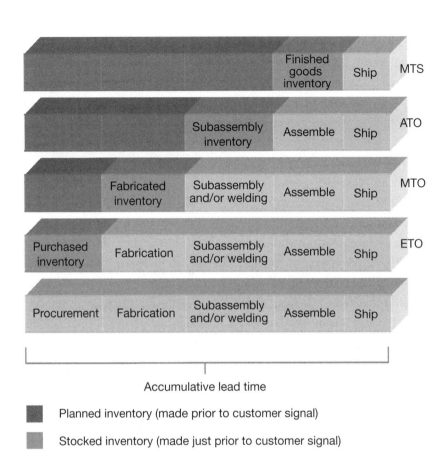

Accumulative lead time

■ Planned inventory (made prior to customer signal)

■ Stocked inventory (made just prior to customer signal)

□ Scheduled activity (scheduled after customer signal)

MTS = Make to stock

ATO = Make to order

MTO = Make to order

ETO = Engineer to order

Figure 5.1 Inventory strategy.

uncommon for companies to have several inventory strategies, with separate pricing and service requirements for each. These decisions are generally linked to product life cycle characteristics.

The reason it is so important to review the inventory strategy is that the planning world revolves around these strategies. Although many companies do not acknowledge this specific thought process, in reality, all companies have to make these decisions. Too many organizations will say they have one inventory strategy and actually are doing something totally different.

I was once called into a company by a friend who had just taken a new position as VP and general manager of an operation that manufactures in Mexico but is headquartered near Los Angeles. My first visit was to the head-quarters, where I met with the top-management staff, VP of engineering, VP of sales, VP of operations, and the president. During the conversations I asked what their inventory strategy was. The president replied, "We are totally a make-to-order company. We do not buy components or start any manufacturing without a firm purchase order or schedule instructions from the customer." I found this interesting because I knew at least one of their customers, Caterpillar, required a two-day lead time. I decided not to argue but instead to wait and see for myself at the plant visit scheduled for the following day. When we arrived at the plant, I was soon able to talk to Dennis, the master scheduler. One of the first questions for Dennis concerned, of course, the inventory strategy. Dennis responded, "We are totally a make-to-order company. We do not buy any components or start any manufacturing without a firm purchase order or schedule instructions from the customer." Sounds familiar, doesn't it?

Further discussion revealed that, in fact, one of their major customers was fair but very demanding. This customer would give forecasts several weeks out in the form of a blanket order. They also gave (semifirm) schedules a couple weeks out but ultimately and predictably gave firm schedule releases from that schedule two days prior to required shipment. The lead time for the supplier process had a 16-week component. This long-lead-time purchased part was a specialized copper element made almost exclusively for their application. They also had a welding process that took a couple days prior to assembly. Assembly took another day.

All of this time belied the statement that this organization was strictly an MTO company. We all know that it can be difficult to have a 16-week lead time item and deliver product in 2 days with an MTO strategy. I asked Dennis about this. He replied, "Well, Caterpillar is a demanding customer. They often change Tuesday's schedule on Monday. We do not want to let them down, so we make extra inventory of the popular configurations and store them on the line in anticipation of these last-minute schedule changes." As I heard this it became obvious that Dennis did not schedule exclusively MTO inventory strategy. Even he was not consciously aware of this reality. By anticipating demand, Dennis was actually doing some MTS (make-to-stock) inventory. This is typical in many organizations.

The lesson here is to acknowledge the process as it exists and change it if it is not appropriate. With the proper acknowledgment, management is more in control of the risks taken and no one gets surprised by inventory that, by design, was built into the process. Inventory strategy affects master scheduling in many ways. Inventory strategies change the method used for master scheduling suppliers and components. This can circle back to the strategies of the business planning process. Recognizing inventory strategy is good policy, but the rules agreed upon internally need to be understood by all the players— what products, how much, and when. Inventory strategy is not designed to say "no" to the customer. Inventory strategy is acknowledged so that everyone in the business is on the same wavelength.

This is not rocket science. No one has to argue about this. When lead time requirements from the customer are shorter than the total accumulative lead time of the supply chain and manufacturing process, some of the process must be planned. See Figure 5.2. That means some of the lead time in the process is committed to via forecasted or planned requirements.

Sometimes, as in the case of this supplier to Caterpillar, a company makes some finished goods in anticipation of the actual customer order. Inventory strategy should be mapped out and agreed to by both the demand- and supply-side management, and the rules of engagement should be documented. When the market or strategy changes, the handshake between the demand- and supply-side parties needs to be updated. Again, the objective is to provide

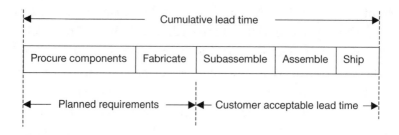

Figure 5.2 Determination of inventory strategy.

the lowest cost with the highest service. To acknowledge the realities of inventory strategy is to allow for the most cost-effective and highest customer service processing of orders.

PRODUCT FAMILIES

The language of the S&OP is product family. Inventory strategy comes into play in this language translation. Let's say that a business named Auto Inc. makes automotive components. This same business sells directly to an OE (original equipment) manufacturer, through aftermarket distribution, and also sells directly to builders for custom hotrod work. Radiators are one of the main products in this imaginary example. Although if this were a real company, there would most likely be several other products/families, for simplicity, we will discuss just one product. The sales forecast for Auto Inc. is stated in total units for the radiator end-item product family. Within this family are several configurations, some with long lead times, others with less. Planning capacity and component availability for a product family such as this example becomes complex when lead time and inventory position for each vary dramatically.

A better S&OP process decision is for this company to take the product family definition to one more level of detail using the inventory strategy as an important part in the designations. As mentioned, radiators are one of the main products manufactured at Auto Inc. This facility might want to have one product family for MTS radiators in anticipation of the OE orders and another product family for the MTO product for the aftermarket distribution,

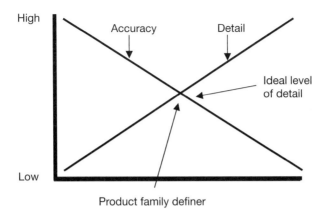

Figure 5.3 Accuracy versus detail comparison.

where you expect the inventory to be carried, and maybe even a third ETO product family for the low-volume custom product supplied to the hotrod builders.

At this level of detail, in most cases we do not violate the handshake suggested in Figure 5.3. In this diagram we are reminded of the realities of defining product groupings for the S&OP process. Choosing the right level of detail for the families is not an exact science, but there are lessons learned by those who have gone before that are worthy of attention. Acknowledging inventory strategy will help companies divide the products into product families to make them manageable segments for the S&OP process.

The detail/accuracy plot in the figure is repeated from Chapter 4 because it is so important to acknowledge. By defining families in our example as MTS radiators, MTO radiators, and ETO radiators, we also change the demand planning requirements and the business planning requirements. *Cardinal rule: In Class A ERP or high-performance S&OP application, all top-management planning processes (business planning, demand planning, and operations planning) must be designated and measured in the exact same product family designations.* That means the business planning families are equal to the demand planning families and are equal to the operations planning families. This way there is little confusion about what certain inventory scheduling methodologies cost and how much margin they are producing.

ELEMENTS OF OPERATIONS PLANNING

Following are a few elements of operations planning worthy of discussion.

Elements of Operations Planning

1. Rough-cut capacity planning—Internal
   - Capital equipment
   - Factory locations
   - Factory capacity
2. Supply chain capacity—External
3. Detailed resource planning
   - People
   - Skills
   - Machinery capacity—Short term
   - Plant capacity—Short term
4. Objectives planning in support of the business plan
5. Measurements

ROUGH-CUT CAPACITY PLANNING

Operations planning is the culmination of all the responsibilities of the supply side of the business. There should be great respect for all successful vice presidents of operations throughout the world. Success does not normally come from luck. Some would say that these VPs do not always get the respect they deserve. Getting it right isn't always a walk in the park. Operations planning done correctly means having the right products in place when the customer needs them. Operations planning requires the right skills, the right machinery, the right capacity, and the right process at the right time—no small task. That is why the best operations professionals have sound management systems and use measurement as a window on process proficiency and predictability.

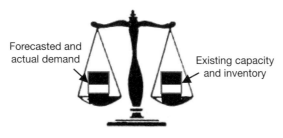

Balancing existing capacity and inventory
with forecasted and actual demand

Figure 5.4 Operations planning.

Rough-cut capacity planning starts with the overall strategic plan and overlaps with the 12-month rolling demand plan. Having these plans in the same shared product family designations is helpful for the planning process—especially with regard to machinery and plant capacity issues. The strategic element of rough-cut capacity planning is simply the assurance that the business is set with plants and equipment for the three- to five-year plans. Knowing that a new plant will be brought online in less than two years will normally affect decisions throughout the business. Also, adding (or shutting down) plants is normally not a 12-month process, and looking ahead is the only sane way of approaching this monumental task. It is impossible to do a good job of rough-cut capacity planning without linking it to the supply chain expectations. See Figure 5.4.

By using both a good planning process involving handshakes with the demand side of the organization and good data gathering, the task of rough-cut capacity planning becomes doable. The questions are not complicated:

- Does your organization have enough plant capacity to produce product to meet the long-term strategic plan?

- Does your organization have enough machine capacity and people to support the plant needs?

- Are the plants in the right location to meet customer demands as forecasted by the strategic plan?

There are no shortcuts in this space. Risk management and good business savvy are prescribed here. This is the responsibility of top management, however. It can't be delegated down the organization effectively. Ignoring rough-cut capacity planning is not an option in high-performance, growing businesses. Lean manufacturing requires quick reflexes. Anticipation of customer moves is very helpful in managing for flexibility.

SUPPLY CHAIN CAPACITY

Very few companies have been able to survive, following Henry Ford's early model, by maintaining a completely vertically designed manufacturing process flow. In Henry's early days, iron ore was taken from the mines owned by Ford and processed, machined, welded, and assembled into automobiles completely within the ownership and watchful eye of the Ford organization. This level of vertical integration is rare today. Most companies just find it too difficult to be the best at all processes involved in the complete product manufacturing and rely on other specialists for some components or processes. This can include plating, heat treating, or even component purchases. Good conscience, regulations, and environmental laws have also made it difficult to finance environmentally friendly and regulation-compliant equipment amortized on just the equipment's own manufacturing requirements. It often requires multiple customers to afford the capital equipment. This has led to supply chain dependency.

To make matters worse, as is well understood in all markets, the introduction of a global market has complicated the equation even more. Now low-cost regions and improved quality and transportation have facilitated the movement of supply chain legs to areas very far away, often on the other side of the globe. High-performance organizations today are as cognizant of their suppliers' capacity as they are their own. Critical operations and company material flow are dependent on these suppliers providing a continuous stream of parts flow almost regardless of what normal process variation is thrown at them. Capacity confirmation needs to happen not only through metrics but also through regular scheduled visits and phone discussions. This needs to happen at a relatively high level within both organizations. With the top

Table 5.1 Capacity Plan for Manpower Resources for Product Family A

	Jan	Feb	Mar	Apr	May	Jun	Jul	Aug	Sep	Oct	Nov	Dec
(All units and hours in thousands)												
Forecast in units	43	54	55	56	78	76	65	55	51	44	54	45
Req'd manpower hrs.	215	270	275	280	390	380	325	275	255	220	270	225
Existing manpower	280	280	280	280	280	280	280	280	280	280	280	280
Delta in hours	65	10	5	0	-110	-100	-45	5	25	60	10	55

managers involved, there is more likely to be appreciation for critical expenditures or actions required by the people who can govern these decisions.

DETAILED RESOURCE PLANNING

The detailed requirements for operations planning are different from the rough-cut requirements in that they are shorter term and much more granular. The areas of concern are (1) manpower, (2) skill sets, and (3) machinery and plant capacity. In each case, high-performance organizations will understand as best they can both expected need and existing resources. It is impossible to be totally prepared for a successful S&OP without understanding the details, especially in areas of capacity constraints or risks.

Detailed Resource Planning—Manpower

In the case of manpower, most organizations have a ratio (by product family) of manpower requirements, per unit. (See Table 5.1.) These ratios can be applied to the forecast and calculations made for pending requirements in future periods. This is yet another reason to do all the S&OP planning within the same product family designators. By taking the demand plan by product family and time-phasing the requirements, the schedulers can see any gaps that need to be dealt with in the future. The idea is to know about these gaps in time to effectively deal with them in a cost-effective manner. When the forecast is applied to the existing resource acknowledgment, actions can then be taken as necessary. These actions might include scheduling overtime, scheduling temporary employees for certain periods, or, in the other direction, promoting vacation use in a certain time period or asking for volunteers to take time off.

Detailed Resource Planning—Skill Sets

Skill requirements are an important component within capacity planning. After all, people counts only work if the counts are flexible to the requirements. Skill sets are a little less mathematical and need to be thoughtfully dealt with for sustainable high performance. Skill, in most businesses, is a much more important capacity requirement today than it was a few years ago. Technology has replaced back-breaking work, and computers have replaced some skills and at the same time created requirements for new ones. For example, McDonald's does not necessarily have to have clerks skilled in arithmetic because the POS (point-of-sale) terminals are fairly foolproof. When clerks press the key for a Quarter Pounder, the cost is automatically entered and displayed. When they punch in the amount of money received from the customer, the POS terminal then tells the clerks exactly how much change to give back to the customer. Instead of arithmetic skills, McDonald's has the added need for IT (information technology) resources and skills.

Manufacturing businesses have similarly migrating skills. Understanding this is important and the responsibility of management, including first-line and middle managers in the organization. Again, the use of a forecast from the demand planning process and an S&OP process is essential to understanding the needs of the coming year. The 12-month rolling demand plan by product family is not only extremely helpful; it is essential.

Detailed Resource Planning—Machinery

The last discussion point within the short-term detail resource planning focus is machinery. Machinery, like people's skill set requirements, is changing continuously with product and process technology. When applied correctly, new technology affects the flexibility, cost, and speed of operations. Capital spending, when used wisely, can help maintain competitive advantage in this regard. Sometimes it is just smart to migrate to new technology for efficiency's sake, even if there are no capacity issues. Keeping abreast of the latest technologies is a good idea regardless of the money available or the need for additional

1-year— Very ideal payback period for most business investments	2-year— Ideal payback period for most business investments	3-year— Reasonable payback period for most business investments	4-year— High payback period for most business investments	5-year— Maximum payback period for most business investments

Figure 5.5 Capital payback period for most high-performance businesses.

capacity. It's probably fair to say that business savvy and awareness are the advantage factors in this space.

There is no magical answer to how much new technology is needed or when, but asking and answering the questions regularly will realize better results. Most companies today are using quite short payback periods for investment. See Figure 5.5. Some companies still use the five-year window, but many have moved to two- or three-year payback justifications. The reasons are twofold: (1) there are a lot of opportunities in most businesses and (2) no one really has a clue as to what will happen in five or six years due to the movement of technology, competition, and market expansion.

In the detailed resource planning space the emphasis is on shorter-term payback periods, whereas the longer-term strategic planning focus normally involves a three- to five-year horizon. See Figure 5.6. There is a different thought process for each. Detailed planning is much more about the day-to-day running of an operation and is linked to the demand plan agreed to and blessed by management in the S&OP process review. The rough cut is a close look in the S&OP to manage upcoming risks. Three- to five-year planning is integrated with market and process changes planned by management in the strategic planning space. While they are always linked, there is a need for focus in both detailed and rough-cut arenas.

Closely linked with the detailed planning discussion on machinery is the plant capacity. Associated with all of the analysis, reviewing the overall short-term outlook for capacity is still important. When looking at the long-term plant capacity, a company must consider such open issues as location, size, and quantity compared to the 12-month rolling plan for capacity, as well as, at times, geographic capacity requirements. The view is mostly internal. This is the planning space where issues like shifts, people numbers, machinery

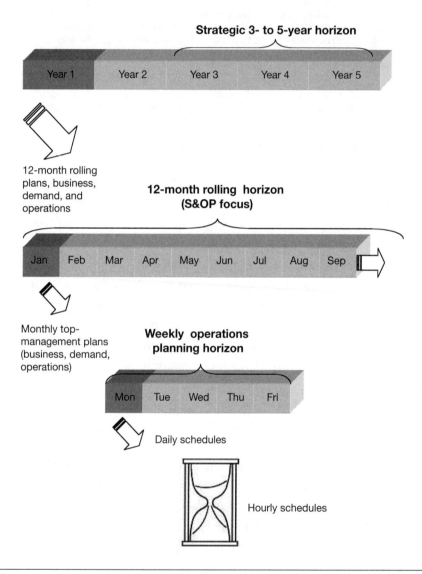

Figure 5.6 Class A ERP planning hierarchy.

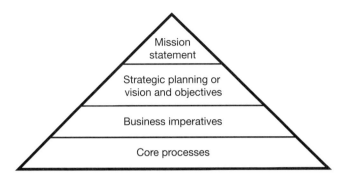

Figure 5.7 Business planning.

capacity short term, and use of temporary resources are evaluated, planned, and/or determined.

OBJECTIVES PLANNING IN SUPPORT OF THE BUSINESS PLAN

Within the business plan elements, goal setting was discussed in Chapter 3. The strategic goals and business imperatives are handed off to the various departments within the organization. The operations group usually ends up with its share of these important goals (often more than its share!). In high-performance organizations these corporate objectives are the lifeblood of performance measurement and often even connected to bonuses. Remember that the definition of business imperative is that "*it will happen in the next 12 months.*"

High-performance operations groups have predictable and repeatable reviews of corporate or company strategy to ensure proper linkage to the objectives within the division. Predictable means that these events are the same time and day of every period. As mentioned in an earlier chapter, this allows employees to know ahead of time when reviews or other events will occur without relying on getting a certain memo or e-mail. There is often a similar approach at each major organizational level within the company or corporate level, meaning there are both operations division strategic objectives and operations business imperatives. All these objectives must link to the corporate imperatives and strategic objectives. Figure 5.7 also appeared in

Figure 5.8 Operations planning.

Chapter 3 but is repeated here so the reader can review it with regard to this discussion.

This model is still appropriate at the operations level. The subordinate operations objectives are specific to the division. The operations equivalent might look more like Figure 5.8.

The hierarchy is essential to keep the objectives linked properly. The real value-add initially is choosing the right objectives, not always a mistake-proof exercise, but without an S&OP management system, even if your savvy has allowed you to pick the right objectives, value is not always harvested. Class A ERP and/or a robust S&OP process and management system structure work well to integrate goals with the project management process.

Operations management should meet at least once a year to formally plan these objectives and align with the corporate vision. In many companies this starts with an analysis just before the corporate strategic session. This helps to ensure operations management is prepared for the top-level assessment coming. After the corporate strategic session, it is the right time to get back together to evaluate current position in relation to any changes that may have happened at the corporate level. It also prepares the VP of operations for the strategic session and gives him or her a good chance to update the rest of the staff on any pertinent discussions from that important annual corporate meeting. If all of these strategy and objectives meetings are on the respective same day each year, no one misses because of vacation, is caught off-guard, or is not prepared for the meeting when he or she gets there. Once the strategic plan is finalized by the corporate top-management team, the follow-up operations meeting is the gathering where the operational business imperatives are determined. Sometimes these are simply carryovers from the corporate session; other times there are additional imperatives that need to be addressed to meet other needs specific to the operation. This might include training, additional capacity investments, or the transfer of operations from one plant to another for efficiency or cost reduction. It is good to know these imperatives if the right resources and priorities are to be engaged through the S&OP process.

OPERATIONS' PART IN THE S&OP PROCESS

It needs to be said that the main responsibility and expectation from the operations function are capacity, quality, low cost, flexibility, and responsiveness. This is a tall order. This requires a robust execution of the ERP business model and sound management systems. The S&OP process is the culmination of the full forces of operations represented in a commitment that covers costs, inventory, and customer service. Realistically, operations has a great load to carry and is worthy of it when Class A ERP processes, including the S&OP processes, are in place.

PROCESS OWNERSHIP IN OPERATIONS PLANNING

Process ownership in operations is not difficult to determine. The top manager in the manufacturing division is the process owner. This is usually the vice president of operations. In larger companies where there are separate operations for Asia, South America, Europe, and so on, there often is a separate S&OP initiative in each region. This leaves process ownership to the ranking operations manager in each region. Process ownership means taking responsibility for the metric and process performance. It includes accuracy of capacity plans committed to and executed monthly. These plans of record are documented in the monthly S&OP review.

In a robust ERP process there are many more processes subservient to the operations planning process and each has a specific ownership and accountability. These are not to be confused with top-management planning process ownership. Accountability of the top manager in operations happens at the general manager, president, or CEO level and is evident at the S&OP review and other project management and performance reporting events at the top level.

OPERATIONS PLANNING MEASUREMENT

The performance measurement for the operations process is simple and straightforward. As you can see in Table 5.2, the metric is strictly evaluated by product family. The tendency to look only at overall units produced (total volume) is tempting but not in the spirit of the ERP and S&OP process effort. This is one reason that product families have to be common throughout the planning process.

The metric calculation is posted and reported as the average accuracy per product family. Some mathematicians and even engineers will get nervous about this approach, as it is realistically an "average of averages." While true, this is the way it needs to be. The calculation in this example is (98 percent + 99 percent + 100 percent + 94 percent + 99 percent) / 5, or 98 percent performance. Notice that the metric also observes the absolute deviation from plan in each product family. In product family D there were 8500 produced, with a plan of 8000 units. Family E has a similar situation. There was a reason for this miss, and the metric points toward finding that root cause. Remember that to achieve high-performance or Class A levels of ERP performance, there needs to be both good planning and good execution. When the plan is outperformed, sometimes it is simply a result of bad planning. When the metric points out inaccuracy, it can be addressed and the organization can learn from it. It must be this way. The spirit of Class A ERP is to have predictable processes and performance. Cost and inventory levels are usually critical for meeting company objectives. It is important to have both plans and execution highly accurate.

I may regret these next few paragraphs. I am about to reveal a trade secret . . . at least from my viewpoint. Many of you will be saying to yourselves as you read the metric calculation that in *your* business, product family designators are so unequal that your recommendation will be to *weight* the values in line

Table 5.2 Operations Planning Metric

	(All units in thousands)		
	S&OP Commitment in units	**Actual in units**	**Performance**
Product family A	90	92	98%
Product family B	50	49	99%
Product family C	78	78	100%
Product family D	8	8.5	94%
Product family E	155	157	99%
Total performance			**98%**

with monthly volumes. In effect, the result will no longer be the "average" accuracy per product family.

If you are the S&OP implementation champion or team leader, I would recommend you heed many years of experience. In the beginning of the Class A implementation, *do not* weight the values. It only hides lessons that benefit the organization long term. Remember that the objective is high performance, not "95s in boxes." If that is your attitude, you will see the point of this argument. If the organization is serious about root cause and uses the metrics to learn and drive change, the lessons that are learned will be valuable. Here is my trade secret: After the performance is in the 90s and the business is in a much more sound position from the standpoint of understanding process variation and reasons for inaccurate plans, there is less risk in adjusting the numbers and weighting *can be* more appropriate. During Class A ERP implementations, I normally insist on straight averages until the team has worked the root causes to a reasonable level of understanding and performance. I don't normally talk about this reprieve from averages in the beginning and have now let the cat out of the bag.

There are actually a couple more "cats" to release. There *can* be exceptions to this rule. If there are, for example, small product families that truly are differentiated from the rest of the normal build, there may be a need for weighting from the start. For example, one client has a kitting operation that shares no capacity nor any components with other operations. It is truly a stand-alone but small process. This product family represents less than 1 percent of the business. Five other product families share the balance of 99 percent, ranging between 8 percent and 33 percent. The only family that is weighted on volume is the small kitting family. Whatever you do in this regard, make sure you go after the root cause of each family and eliminate the reasons for process variation. The kinds of process interruptions experienced in one family, even a small one, will usually be helpful in the whole business. The more that weighting is applied, the less effort will be applied to the small families. Don't fall into this trap. Enough said.

The operations planning process is arguably the heartbeat of any organization. Although sales will argue their importance is second to none, without operations, it is pretty difficult to meet customer need. Getting this process right is worth the effort. The S&OP process, along with the accountability associated with it, will help greatly to shine a light on the weaknesses of the process and the root causes of those opportunities.

∗ ∗ ∗ ∗

6

THE S&OP
MEETING STRUCTURE

The meeting structure should be consistent at each S&OP meeting. This allows all process owners to know exactly what to expect and to come prepared with their homework done, ready to reconcile gaps in performance and to share learning. This top-management gathering, which happens every month, should adhere to the agenda outline in Figure 6.1.

S&OP STANDARD AGENDA

1. *Review of last 30 days*—The accuracy metrics by product family are reviewed.

   a. *Review financial plan accuracy by product family*—The top-management financial manager (usually the CFO) communicates root-cause analysis of any process variation and actions to improve upcoming accuracy. Because in many businesses the books are not yet closed for the month at the time of the S&OP, the numbers are often built from averages—average cost of units per product family and average revenue per unit from the same product families. These estimates can be

S&OP agenda outline
- Review last 30 days
  - o   Review financials
  - o   Review demand plan accuracy by product family
  - o   Review operations plan accuracy by product family
- Review 30- to 60-day risks in detail as required by product family
  - o   Review financial risks
  - o   Review demand plan risks
  - o   Review operations plan risks
- Review 90- to 120-day risks as required
  - o   Review financial risks
  - o   Review demand plan risks
  - o   Review operations plan risks
- Review balance of 12-month horizon (exception only)
  - o   Review financial risks
  - o   Review demand plan risks
  - o   Review operations plan risks

Figure 6.1 S&OP agenda outline.

compared to forecast margin or gross profit. This is another reason to make sure the product families are the right ones. If there are big swings in cost or price within the family, it may make sense to reevaluate the family groupings.

By defining the families correctly and having the spreadsheets available for analysis during the S&OP, management can make better decisions regarding capacity changes or inventory investments. After all, profit is why everybody is at the meeting! When and if the actual numbers available later after the closing do not match, again, great learning can happen as a result. It is always good to know that estimating is not accurate and why.

b. *Review demand plan accuracy by product family*—The top-management demand-side manager (usually either the VP of sales or the VP of marketing) shares the performance measurement of the demand plan accuracy just prior to communicating root-cause analysis from process variation affecting the performance. This plan is especially interesting to the organization for several reasons. Not only does the forecast tell what inventory and capacity to position; it also time-phases this plan over the next 12 months. The demand plan does not stop there.

Regardless of inventory strategy, the revenue plans are always tied to the demand plan. Make-to-stock demand plans suggest the demand from stock. In a make-to-order environment, the demand plan lays out the expectations of increases to backlog that drive the operations plan. This operations plan in an MTO environment or product family is the revenue plan. In MTO, the plant builds what the customer ordered and it normally ships soon with consolidation of orders or ships as soon as it is built. It becomes easy to understand the interest in this plan.

c. *Review production or operations plan accuracy by product family*—The top operations management manager (usually the VP of operations) communicates the performance measure of the capacity fulfillment plan and the root-cause analysis of process variation made visible through the measurements. Actions are the resulting report aimed at improving upcoming accuracy for any shortfalls. As stated previously, the operations plan is the revenue plan in any MTO product families. Obviously the revenue plan is of high interest.

Almost as important is the risk management associated with the operations plan. This includes the introduction of new products, new suppliers or plants, or even new machine lines. All of these projects represent significant risks to the business if not managed properly. This agenda item in the S&OP welcomes the scrutiny of these risk opportunities with the hope that with the right attention, fewer mistakes or oversights will happen. See Figure 6.2.

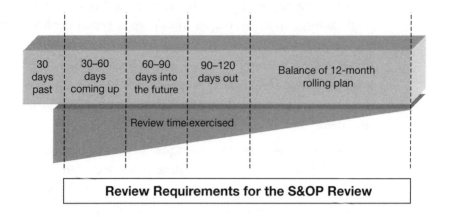

Figure 6.2 Review expectations for the S&OP.

2. *Review of the 30- to 60-day plan expectations*—During this agenda item, risks and/or changes since the last monthly meeting are reviewed in detail.

   a. *Discuss financial plan risks*—Of course, there can be financial risks on the radar screen as well as new changes in financial plans since the last review. The close-in, one- to three-month horizon normally involves risk. This time frame often overlays promises made by the top-management team to outside stakeholders and customers. This, along with the short lead time to fix any issues, leaves this span in time a critical execution horizon and one that needs to have logjams removed quickly when identified.

   b. *Discuss demand plan forecast risks*—With demand so closely associated with revenue, there should be little question about the importance of looking out 30 to 90 days with a high level of scrutiny. Most companies that are focused on growth realize that increases in demand require one of two actions to happen: (1) get existing customers to buy more or (2) get new customers. If growth is predicted, corresponding actions regarding new or existing customers should be reviewed. The importance of these actions in the next 30 to 90 days is obvious to all. The S&OP format does not provide the answers, but it does provide the opportunity to ask the questions and ultimately to find the answers.

c. *Discuss production risks*—In many companies there are probably no more obvious risks than those in operations planning and execution. Along with the obvious risks come the not-so-obvious risks that can slip through the cracks (seemingly too often). These risk opportunities include new product introductions, new machine line implementations, additional new shifts being added, product transfers from one plant to another, and new suppliers coming on board. Explaining these risks in this chapter is likely not necessary; the risks should be obvious. Suffice it to say that anytime a manufacturing facility has a large project that requires several support activities to be coordinated and where there is a financial impact if the dates, quality, or details are not met, it becomes pretty obvious that a management system is of value. The S&OP process is exactly that.

Scott, one of the best plant managers I have worked with and a friend of mine (who asked that his last name be left out), recently asked why plant managers shouldn't be expected to take care of this type of follow-up. "Why does top management need to be involved all the time?" he asks. The answer is simple. Each plant manager has a defined world and his or her own priorities and objectives. These do not always perfectly correspond with other plant managers, and top management can best see this quickly.

When working with AlliedSignal in Europe a few years ago (pre-Honeywell), Bill Amelio, the president of the Transportation and Power Systems (Garrett) division, wanted product to be produced by the most cost-effective plants. This often created situations where product manufacturing would be shifted from one European plant to another because of differences in plant efficiency. This created a healthy competitive

Risk opportunities
1) New product introduction
2) Production line moves
   a. Supplier changes
   b. Production line changes
3) Promotions or marketing events
4) Understanding seasonality or cyclicality
5) Currency exchange risks

Figure 6.3 Common future risk possibilities.

situation, but the receiving plant manager always had a much different perspective than the sending plant manager even though all parties were mature, experienced managers. When top management asked a few appropriate questions as the project approached, the quality of transfer always seemed to improve. The S&OP (they called it SIOP at AlliedSignal) created the forum to make sure the right measures were in place to make smooth transitions. Simply knowing there was a reporting structure at the highest level facilitated better transitions.

3. *Review of the 90- to 120-day plan expectations*—On an exception-only basis, this time frame is detailed. See Figure 6.3.

   a. *Discuss new product introduction for risks of plan accuracy*— This was briefly mentioned in the shorter-term view earlier in the chapter, but new products do not normally just cover the horizon of 30-60-90 days. In fact, often from the point of justification, there can be several weeks or, in some businesses, months before the increases in volume and required capacity are scheduled. There are several important gates that need to be reviewed and quality of actions ensured. When this is done right, companies have a much greater chance of high performance. After all, it is these new products that allow growth from either new customers or additional buys from existing ones.

b. *Discuss production shifts to alternative sources such as moving product lines to offshore sights, supply chain changes and risks, and so on*—The list can be infinite on this topic. All risks should be fair game for the S&OP review.

c. *Review promotions, shows, customer actions, and so forth on an exception-only basis*—Many businesses do not hold planned marketing impact with the same high level of expectation that planned engineering innovation or operations success is held. Marketing events are planned from time to time in most businesses. If these are justified, an expected outcome would be assumed. This impact on demand should be visible and identified on the horizon. The business gets the full benefit of the learning that can happen from each of these with the visibility created in a well-managed S&OP process.

d. *Review/verify normal cyclicality/seasonality*—This does not take long usually when everyone is aware of the normal cycles. In one business that makes dance costumes, the seasonality was severe. Dance recitals are only held in the May/June time frame, making up the bulk of their annual sales. As new products were introduced, the seasonality began to change. Halloween, for example, was an opportunity at the other end of the calendar. Making sure everyone is on the same page is very helpful. The S&OP process review forces this review.

e. *Discuss anticipated currency exchange issues affecting the plan accuracy*—Here is an impact that is often not monitored until it becomes too late and an unfavorable surprise occurs. The top financial manager and the CEO are normally the risk managers in this high-risk category. There is probably no way to always be right on currency futures, but since it affects the bottom line in most global businesses, it should be a topic of review at the S&OP. Although it might not help improve the accuracy, asking the right questions regularly can remind top management of the risks—exactly the reason the S&OP process exists in high-performance businesses.

4. *Quick review of the balance of the 12-month rolling schedule reviewed for anomalies or changes expected*—This agenda item is designed to review exceptions only, making sure there are no unforeseen high-stakes risks in the 12-month rolling plan.

   a. *Communicate any new information*—In most businesses there are anticipated projects linked to either the strategic planning process or the business imperatives. Either can provide opportunities to increase risk in the future months. By maintaining a short list and reviewing it for new information each month at the S&OP meeting, a company can enhance its chances for success. Possible review topics include the following:

      i. New plants being built
      ii. New machines or lines being added to existing plants
      iii. Changes in volumes requiring an additional shift
      iv. New large customer coming onboard or leaving
      v. New market being targeted
      vi. Numerous other risk opportunities

   b. *Review changes from the previous plan*—Perhaps the most efficient way to structure the agenda in the 12-month rolling time frames is to work from an exception-only basis. With efficiency, however, can come danger. Organizations that only discuss the exceptions and do not perform due diligence to determine and avoid trip wires in the future do not get full value from their efforts. If it is easy to miss important risks because of negligence, there can be a steep cost. While there is no magic formula for keeping this future 12-month rolling review at high quality, probably one of the best approaches is to have the functional manager from each area review all risks in his or her space that might occur within a 12-month time frame. This review simply means the question is asked of each functional VP concerning upcoming risks. Honesty will bring the right topics to the floor. In many organizations an ongoing list will remind the organization of specifics like big projects. This project list can be a good follow-up list.

S&OP PROCESS MEETING ATTENDEES

The attendees at the S&OP vary depending on the scope of the S&OP and the size of the organization. In small companies there is often one S&OP that includes all major players in the top-management team. Typically the master scheduler for the company is the person responsible for the spreadsheets prepared for the meeting. The president or CEO is the typical leader of the meeting and process owner for the results of this review. The first topic should always be the performance from the last 30 days. This starts the group on the right foot, acknowledges proper (or improper) planning quality, and heightens the frequency and impact of lessons learned. When top management is not involved, the meeting really cannot be called a true S&OP, because a sales and operations planning function, by design, is a *top-management* planning process.

It is also important to focus on the performance stated in quantitative factual representative data, not just opinions. When dealing only with data and facts and not with emotions or opinions, the group continues to focus on the goals and does not let their guard down unexpectedly. The best managers running an S&OP process keep to the facts. For example, discussion would be focused on the fact that the demand plan was at 87 percent accuracy with a goal of 90 percent—and not on opinions or statements like "the accuracy of the forecast wasn't too bad this month." There is a big difference in these two approaches: Real facts tend to drive more improvement.

At this point in this discussion, the two most important players have been listed, the president and the master scheduler. There are, obviously, several other key players, some of whom have been mentioned in the agenda description. The next player is a very influential and important figure in any manufacturing business, the VP of sales or marketing. The owner of the demand side of the equation, this position is critical in bringing the market voice to the table. To balance the power and influence and complete the handshake in the S&OP, the VP of operations must be listed on the "required" S&OP team. It takes the two sides, demand and supply, to successfully complete the handshake.

There are typically two additional key players in the S&OP meeting structure: the VP of finance or CFO and the VP of engineering. The finance professional has early agenda items reconciling the anticipated results as seen at the end of the month without the books necessarily closed, as well as the plan of record at the beginning of the month. The finance ownership is one of conscience and forethought for the business and less about just reporting yesterday's numbers. This is a change for some financial types. Only a generation ago the finance role consisted more of simply reporting. While a GM at Raymond, I used to remind Jackie Wafer, the division accounting manager, "Telling what happened yesterday doesn't take much talent. The real value from the finance team is to tell us what will happen tomorrow." She frequently got it right.

The VP of engineering can have a varied role in the S&OP process. From a standpoint of meeting structure, the engineering representative is normally there to address risk opportunities with new product development and time schedules involving the same. An extremely important asset to the business, the designs are critical to the timing of the new product introduction and successful market launches. High-performance organizations understand this criticality and manage the new product introduction gates accordingly. See Figure 6.4.

WHEN DOES THE S&OP MEETING HAPPEN?

The S&OP process should be scheduled 12 months in advance and should always be top priority on the schedule. In high-performance organizations, it is very rare to reschedule the S&OP meeting. Frequent requests to reschedule the S&OP process are a sign that there is a prioritization issue and the S&OP process is not winning the battle. Even customers can be managed most of the time to work around this important meeting.

The S&OP review is normally held on the first, second, or third workday of the month. It is good to have it as close to the last workday of the month as possible to maximize the effect on the coming month. The meeting happens every month without exception and normally only holidays are a reason for exception scheduling. Even then, if the formula is around the workday sequence, there will still be a third workday, even if it is delayed due to a major holiday. If there is valid a reason for absence (sickness, death in the family,

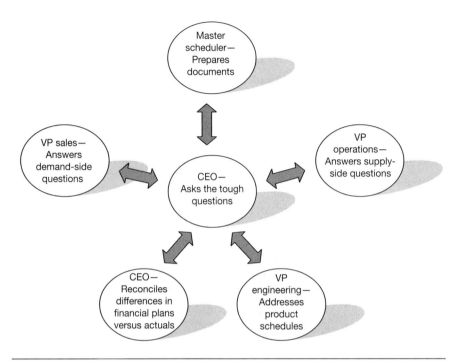

Figure 6.4 Players in the S&OP meeting structure.

unavoidable customer issue, etc.), it is expected that a fully authorized delegate will take appropriate accountability to the meeting in the person's stead. Homework should still be complete and carried by the delegate to explain. This may seem difficult, but if it is an objective of the organization, it is possible.

WHAT HAPPENS IF TOP MANAGEMENT IS UNWILLING TO PRESET SCHEDULES?

There are some organizational cultures that seem not to understand the meaning of prescheduled sessions or meetings that cannot be preempted. I have been involved in a few client cultures like that. Cultures are created by the leadership and the examples they set. There are no perfect answers for situations in this category. After all, the boss is the boss. He or she sets the tone and expectations for the organization, and the rest follow that example. An aid to correcting this situation can be administered through top-management education done by a reputable and respected outside resource. Education and training in the proper implementation and procedures of the S&OP process can do a lot of good for managers that are willing to listen. This is normally a three- or four-hour session dedicated to top-management involvement, their roles and responsibilities, and most importantly, the financial and operational benefits of a robust S&OP process. The syllabus for this education and training typically includes the following:

- What exactly is an S&OP process?
- Why do high-performance companies perform this monthly ritual? What are the benefits?
- Who is involved and what are the roles of the players?
- Who are the process owners?
- What is the timetable for this management system?
- What are the metrics used?
- What are the outputs of this important process?
- What is the formula for successful implementation?

In situations where top management is unwilling to set these meeting schedules in stone, the suggestion is to take whatever schedule is offered and make the best of it. As long as the meeting happens regularly and it is attended by the correct accountable and prepared players, many gains can be had. Many companies implement variations on the "perfect S&OP" and still see many positive effects on their business's performance. There are several right answers. The formula in this book is one of them. It is one that has been proven over several years and in literally hundreds of companies.

Many times, simply getting the spirit or intent of the process well established is enough to enjoy several benefits. By getting the top managers to understand this intent and by measuring the process performance and reviewing a 12-month rolling demand and operating plan, there are always gains through the associated risk management.

* * * *

7

S&OP TOOLS FOR
HIGH PERFORMANCE

As mentioned in an earlier chapter, although numerous good ERP business system tools are available on the market, surprisingly few do an especially good job with the S&OP process. Probably one of the reasons is that it is done so easily on a Lotus- or Excel-type spreadsheet today. Access is also available for the more advanced crowd when S&OP is done on simple, widely used tools. The real truth is that ERP software can sometimes get in the way. Good S&OP process requires nimble and flexible controls. If the product families need to be adjusted because of new pricing strategies, for example, a spreadsheet can be changed in 10 minutes, whereas special software may have to involve someone from IT and may take weeks—if it gets done at all.

There is no reason to feel bad about utilizing spreadsheet technology for the S&OP process. I have worked with hundreds of clients over the years and have yet to have one completely manage their S&OP process on their ERP system. All have used spreadsheets. This is probably not going to change in the near future. Although some of the more sophisticated ERP software programs are getting much better and starting to cater to the needs of S&OP planning processes, most likely most planning processes will not be affected in the next few years. Tool changes happen when the desired state is much better and changing is less painful than staying the course with existing tools.

Spreadsheets just work too well to drive much change in this arena. The opportunity may come to those organizations that are seasoned at S&OP and are in the middle of system choice and/or ERP system conversion. Even if S&OP process becomes easy in formal ERP business systems, it is likely that the spreadsheet format will still be utilized and changes rolled up or down to or from the ERP system. Bottom-line message: Don't let the lack of systems stop your organization from getting this process in place.

Enough said on the topic for now. In this chapter the emphasis will be on simple tools and layouts that help in the planning and analysis for robust S&OP process.

DISPLAYING THE S&OP FOR TOP-MANAGEMENT REVIEW

The first view of the S&OP is probably the entire view by product family. Since the business plan and demand plan are in different units of measure (dollars versus units), it probably will be most helpful to look at each on a separate chart. In this chapter all of the charts will follow data from the following S&OP product family chart. Note that product family XYZ is only one of many (6 to 10) families that would be reviewed in a normal S&OP process. See Table 7.1

The charts are typically 12 rolling months in duration. See Figure 7.1. In the figure, the demand dips in the late summer and comes back at the end of the year. When the entire plan is viewed, sometimes something can jump out and make the discussion and analysis more valuable. The examples in this chapter are January through December, but remember that these are rolling 12-month charts, so the following chart one month later would visually depict February through January of the following year. The first month should always be the current or just-completed month.

Another way to look at the same information is to view it in bar chart form. This is a personal preference issue, but many find bar charts to be friendly for finding errors in the planning process. See Figure 7.2.

Once the full S&OP chart by product family is viewed, the next charts to review are probably the detail charts by category (business plan, demand plan,

Table 7.1 S&OP Family XYZ

	Jan	Feb	Mar	Apr	May	Jun	Jul	Aug	Sep	Oct	Nov	Dec
					All units in thousands							
Demand plan	37	37	38	45	32	29	28	25	25	25	35	34
Operations plan	38	36	37	38	35	34	30	24	24	28	32	36
Backlog	4	5	6	13	10	5	3	4	5	2	5	3

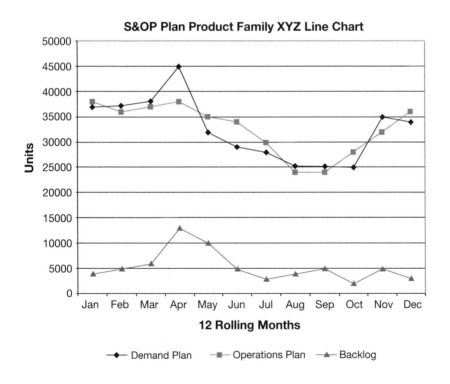

Figure 7.1 S&OP plan for family XYZ.

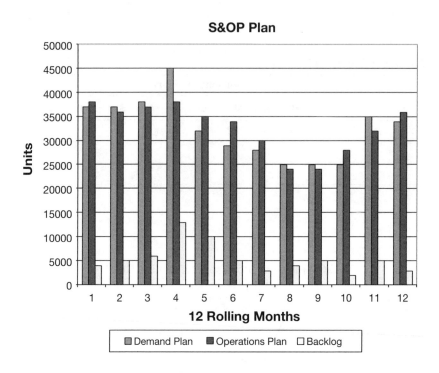

Figure 7.2 Full S&OP by product family—bar chart.

operations plan, backlog, inventory). See Figure 7.3 for an example of the demand plan associated with the full view from Figure 7.1.

Other detail charts are necessary to exercise the full analysis. See Figure 7.4 for an example of product family XYZ business plan (in this case it is profit).

The operations plan is often the most controllable adjustment knob in the business. The operations plan is typically the most scrutinized plan of the deck. See Figure 7.5.

Backlog in make-to-order families is the main driver for lead time to the customer and rates of product-to-cash conversions. For this reason the backlog is a primary objective for MTO families. See Figure 7.6.

The operations plan can be affected by other product families in the facility and is often also viewed from the overall perspective. Table 7.2 shows all of the data from product families in the example company.

Figure 7.7 shows what the data might look like when viewed in one chart. This can provide a total-capacity view that can outline additional risks.

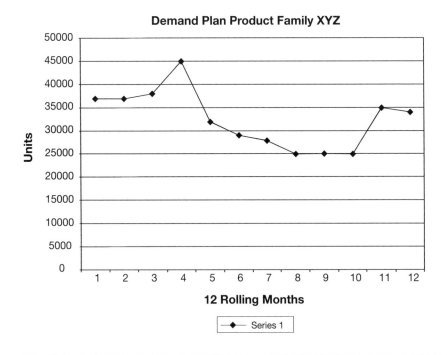

Figure 7.3 Demand plan for family XYZ.

If the capacity for the department that makes product family XYZ was known and displayed, top management would have additional visibility to required actions. Putting this capacity line on the chart management will provide a better feel for the risks in the plan. See Table 7.3 and Figure 7.8.

It becomes quite obvious where the value is in the capacity charts if the plan was a little different. In Figure 7.9, the capacity requirements outgrow the actual demonstrated capacity.

Obviously, action would have to take place in the company that had this chart to review during the S&OP meeting. It needs to be said that, in reality, the master scheduler would have brought this to the attention of the management staff long before this chart would be shown. Nonetheless, the value of looking at the 12-month rolling plan is real. Many companies would wait until the problem was upon them before acting. Done correctly, the S&OP process eliminates those costly mistakes.

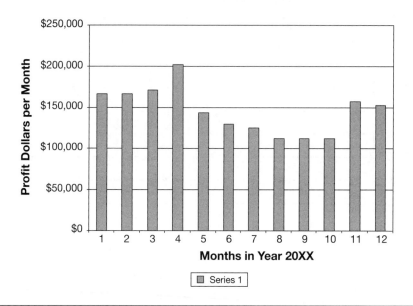

Figure 7.4 Business plan for product family XYZ.

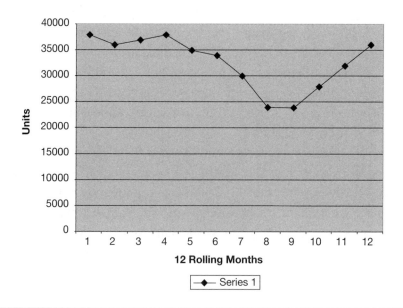

Figure 7.5 Operations plan for product family XYZ.

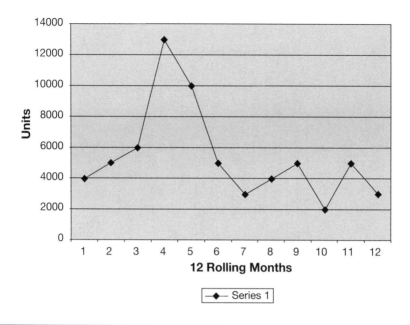

Figure 7.6 Backlog chart.

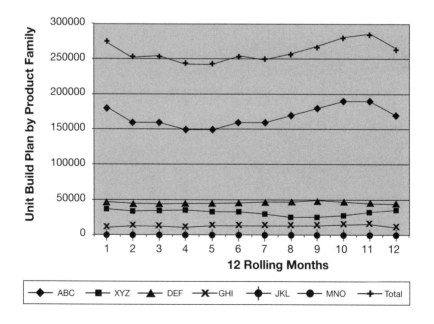

Figure 7.7 All product family operations plans.

Table 7.2 All Product Family Operations Plans

	Jan	Feb	Mar	Apr	May	Jun	Jul	Aug	Sep	Oct	Nov	Dec
ABC	180000	160000	160000	150000	150000	160000	160000	170000	180000	190000	190000	170000
XYZ	38000	36000	37000	38000	35000	34000	30000	24000	24000	28000	32000	36000
DEF	45000	43000	43000	44000	44000	45000	46000	47000	47000	46000	45000	45000
GHI	12000	14000	13000	12000	14000	14000	14000	15000	15000	16000	17000	12000
JKL	100	90	90	90	80	80	90	90	100	90	95	100
MNO	89	67	75	80	120	130	90	80	60	60	60	70
Total	275189	253157	253165	244170	243200	253210	250180	256170	266160	280150	284155	263170

Table 7.3 Capacity and Operations Plan, Family XYZ

	All units in thousands											
	Jan	Feb	Mar	Apr	May	Jun	Jul	Aug	Sep	Oct	Nov	Dec
Operations Plan	38	36	37	38	35	34	30	24	24	28	32	36
Capacity	38	38	38	38	38	38	38	38	38	38	38	38

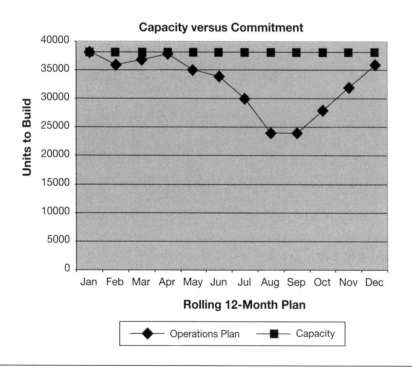

Figure 7.8 Capacity and operations plan, family XYZ.

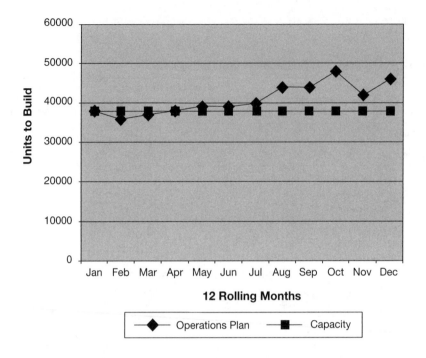

Figure 7.9 Plan exceeds actual capacity.

OTHER VIEWS THAT CAN BE VERY HELPFUL

In larger companies there can often be multiple plants with the same products produced. This is especially true in products where freight is a big expense item and geographic demand is most cost-effectively produced in the corresponding area. Examples are inexpensive products that take up a lot of truck space when shipped. Often these companies have several smaller facilities around the country to manufacture the items in the right geographic area. When plants are viewed together on shared formats and charts, better questions can sometimes be generated by the reviewing management team. The better the questions in the S&OP, the better the process quality and corresponding results will be. See Figure 7.10.

The cost of producing the product is a direct derivative of the business planning process and is very important in the S&OP review. A tool that is

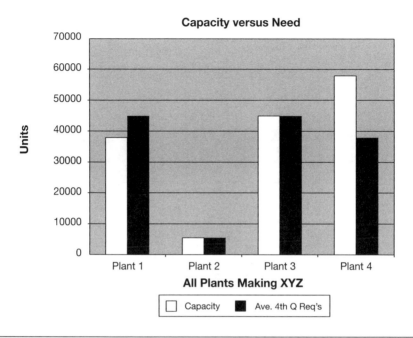

Figure 7.10 Plant capacity and build plan comparison.

often used in this review is a plant-to-plant comparison. One way is to look at cost as a percent of sales. See Figure 7.11.

Another helpful way to look at this cost is by total cost. This includes labor, material, overhead and SGA (sales and general administrative) costs—in other words, everything minus taxes and profit. See Figure 7.12.

Many organizations bring other charts to the S&OP review to help management understand the issues and opportunities. After all, this meeting is one of the most powerful and influential meetings a company can hold, and it is good to have all the data. Data fall into categories that are tied directly to the S&OP or tied to the operational excellence. These extra data are examples of having the homework done and are extremely helpful in making the best decisions possible.

Class A ERP and the Associated Metrics

Class A ERP is a celebrated performance level of the ERP business systems within a manufacturing or service company with specific criteria. Class A ERP

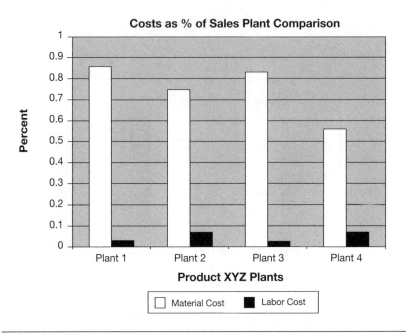

Figure 7.11 Cost comparison, plant to plant, family XYZ.

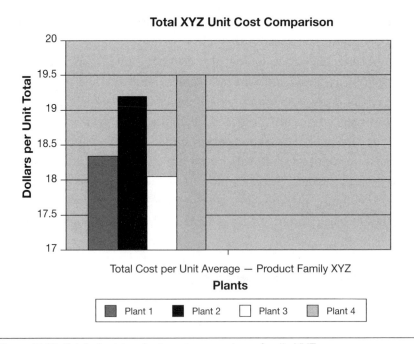

Figure 7.12 Total plant-to-plant cost comparison, family XYZ.

actually incorporates the S&OP process as the top end of the ERP business model in the required criteria. When manufacturing companies are focused on Class A ERP performance as a strategic goal, the metrics involved with Class A ERP are also often reviewed at the session in addition to the standard S&OP measures. These additional Class A ERP metrics are good indicators of operational health beyond—or perhaps better stated, underneath—the S&OP measures. See Figure 7.13.

In Class A ERP environments the measurement process is a top priority with the management team and a strong component of the cultural fiber of the organization. Class A ERP can actually help in the success of the S&OP— not because this top-management review process depends on the Class A ERP measures but because the Class A ERP disciplines and habits drive the right thinking, with their emphasis on continuous improvement, lots of indicators being monitored, and improved performance. These additional ERP measures also shore up the disciplines, making the operations plan much more predictable. This is the thinking upon which good S&OP is built.

For reference only, listed below are the Class A ERP measures. The top-management measures in Class A ERP criteria are exactly the same as the S&OP measures. This is not a coincidence.

1. *Business plan*—Accuracy of the monthly profit plan of the business by product family. If the facility is a cost center, the accuracy of the budget becomes the base for accuracy. (Monthly)

2. *Demand plan (forecast)*—Accuracy of the monthly demand forecast by product family. (Monthly)

3. *Operations plan*—Accuracy of the monthly capacity plan by product family. (Monthly)

4. *Master schedule*—Accuracy of the weekly detailed schedule by line. (Weekly)

5. *Material plan*—Percent of orders that are released with full lead time to suppliers. This is measured against the current lead time field in the item master. (Weekly)

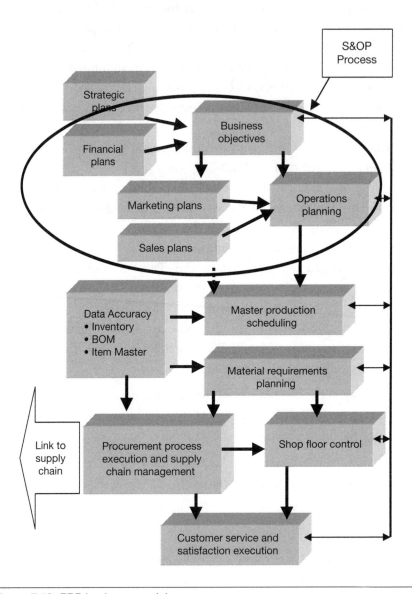

Figure 7.13 ERP business model.

6. *Schedule stability*—Percent of orders that have completion dates revised within the fixed-period time fence. (Weekly)

7. *Inventory location balance accuracy*—Percent of location balances that are perfect. (Daily)

8. *Bill of material accuracy*—Percent of bills of material that are perfect. (Daily)

9. *Item master file accuracy*—Accuracy percentage of other item master fields that come up during the initial assessment of Class A ERP weaknesses. This can include routing records, lead time records, cost standards, and so on. (Daily)

10. *Procurement process accuracy*—Percent of complete orders that are received from suppliers on the day (or hour) currently scheduled in the ERP business system. (Daily)

11. *Shop floor control accuracy*—Percent of complete orders that are completed on the day (or hour) currently scheduled in the ERP business system. (Daily)

12. *First-time quality*—Percent of units that make it through a process without exception handling, movement, or rework. (Daily)

13. *Safety*—Lost-time accidents actual compared to plan. Minimum acceptable is company objective plus improvement. (Daily)

14. *Customer service*—Percent of complete orders that ship to the customer on the original promise date. (Daily)

Because the S&OP process is such an important element within the Class A ERP business model, it is worthy of a second look when one is considering the implementation of a robust top-management planning process.

Other Measures

Some companies add additional process vision to their S&OP process such as project review, operational measurement review, Class A ERP metric review,

CIP (continuous improvement project) review, CAT (corrective actions team) review, and quality review. There are many ways to take advantage of having top managers all in a room at the same time every month. This depends totally on the appetite of top management. The danger here is the dilution of the real spirit of the S&OP process itself. It is better to not do all the other reviews than to miss the real value of the S&OP.

* * * *

8

ROLES IN THE
S&OP PROCESS

Without roles being properly understood and staffed, it is difficult to bring consistency to this important process called the S&OP. Probably no more important role exists than the top manager of the facility. In the case of smaller companies, this might be the president or CEO, and in larger organizations, this role can be populated by plant managers, the COO, a division GM, or, of course, the president or CEO. In this chapter the specific roles are outlined, with emphasis on not only the expectation of responsibility but also S&OP behavioral traits that pay back results quicker. Since there are some obvious differences between small companies and larger ones in terms of roles, the first review covers the needs and roles of larger companies.

PARTICIPANTS IN THE S&OP AND THEIR ROLES IN LARGER MULTIPLANT ENVIRONMENTS

There can be a few variations in participation and roles depending on the organizational structure and size of the business in question. Two views are used as examples in this template, the first being a larger multiplant environment. The example typical of smaller businesses follows. These views are meant as guidelines only and food for thought. It would be impossible to dictate the organizational requirements for S&OP for every company in one book. Nonetheless, these guidelines will be close and will establish a foundation that most companies can find useful.

In a larger organization often product managers are responsible for overall product success, including factors such as the creation of demand, product cost, and overall profitability. It is a highly responsible job, and although they are not always considered top management, they really are solidly in the core of people influencing the business planning process. Larger organizations also often have a demand manager position within either the sales or marketing leg of the business. The demand manager typically reports directly to the VP of sales, the VP of marketing, or in yet other companies the VP of sales *and* marketing. Again, this depends on the size and scope of an organization. In this example the following organizational structure core lineup is used:

1. CEO

2. CFO

3. VP of sales and marketing

4. VP of operations

5. Product managers (one for each product family)

6. Master scheduler

Figure 8.1 depicts the S&OP participants with these organizational assumptions. Note that in this example there is no demand manager; the forecasting process is executed through the product managers.

PARTICIPANTS IN THE S&OP IN SMALLER BUSINESSES

In smaller organizations there are generally fewer top managers, each wearing multiple hats. Because of this, participation in the S&OP engages a smaller group, but the duties are all still required and executed. In smaller businesses a product manager may not exist for each product family. Instead, there might be a demand manager position managing the entire database for product demand. The demand manager normally reports to the ranking demand-side manager and collects data from the field and consolidates input information

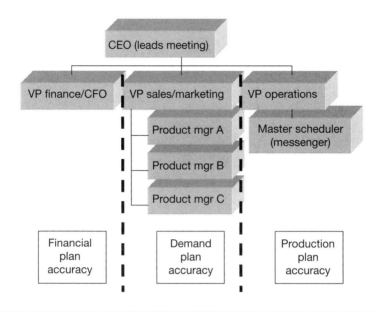

Figure 8.1 Typical participation in the S&OP (larger businesses).

to develop and maintain the demand forecast. This position was described in Chapter 4, "Creating the Demand Plan." Figure 8.2 depicts the typical S&OP participation in such an organization.

Very small organizations do not normally have demand managers. This does not stop the process, but the duties have to be picked up by the sales or marketing administration. In some organizations the responsibilities are filled by having the clerical duties picked up by the administrative assistant to the top demand-side manager, and the analysis done directly by the vice president of sales and marketing. No one scenario is better than another; it simply depends on the complexity of the market, the number of products, the appetite of the VP of sales, and the size of the organization. For a more exacting list of duties for a typical S&OP, the following text generalizes the S&OP process roles for both big and small organizations.

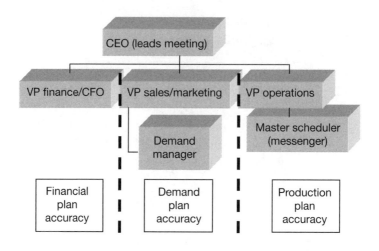

Figure 8.2 Typical participation in the S&OP (smaller businesses).

ROLES IN THE S&OP MEETING

The monthly S&OP meeting in a high-performance organization has a very predictable agenda and clear roles for the players. First, the meeting belongs to the CEO or president, whoever is in charge regularly day to day. This monthly meeting is a main element of the high-performance or Class A ERP management system and, accordingly, accountability needs to be a top priority for this review. Accountability does not mean bloodletting is a required practice at the event. Instead, it means that process owners come into the meeting prepared with their homework done and present the facts, including actions to offset process variation. Accountability is best ensured if there is someone to play the role of asking the tough questions. That role resides with the chair of this meeting, the president or CEO. Each of the other plans (demand plan, operations plan, inventory plan, financial business plan) has a process owner, and it is the role of each owner to propose updates or changes to his or her plan to help eliminate process variation or inaccuracies.

The duties of each in the meeting are described in the following text. Some alternative participants are also listed. Every organization will be a little different in its choice of structure. There is no right or wrong organization

1. Enforces the meeting schedules.
2. Chairs the S&OP.
3. Provides prioritization of actions.
4. Keeps attendance high.
5. Maintains a consistent agenda.
6. Shows accountability at the meeting.
7. Ensures follow-up actions are documented and distributed.

Figure 8.3 The role of the president/CEO in S&OP.

chart as long as the right process owners are accountable for the accuracy and facts surrounding same.

Duties of Each Process Owner in the Monthly S&OP Meeting

President/CEO (See Figure 8.3)

The president, obviously, is the most important player in the business and is also the most important player in the S&OP process. Without the president's support and cooperation, the effectiveness of the process becomes very difficult. Very few "grassroots" S&OP processes are fully effective, since the process is about top-management ownership of risk management. Here are some of the specific S&OP roles and duties of the top manager:

- *Determining and enforcing meeting schedule*—The president maintains the meeting schedule 12 months in advance. This is usually done by always, for instance, holding it on the first Tuesday of every month, or second workday of every month, or some related predictable calculation. If the president takes an active role in keeping the meeting schedule predictable, one of the key elements of success, attendance, is minimized as a process flaw. When everybody knows the meeting schedule way ahead of time, it is less likely for players to have schedule conflicts, especially if the president is always known for his or her attendance at this review.

- *Serving as meeting chair*—It is the expectation that the president will lead the S&OP meeting each month. In most high-performance applications, the president follows a standard agenda, allowing all players to know exactly what to expect and therefore to come prepared with the answers required. The meeting should set the right tone by always starting on time and by sticking to the agenda and not allowing off-focus discussions to get too far out of line. Homework is expected to be both anticipated and complete. Homework consists of preparation for any anticipated questions from the top manager regarding plan accuracy or risks in the future within his or her process ownership realm.

- *Setting prioritization of activity*—The president must ensure that the S&OP meeting is not preempted by other priorities. This can be difficult, and only the president or CEO can pull this off effectively. There are, in most businesses, a multitude of distractions that can happen daily from several sources such as stakeholders or customers. There must be an understanding that this meeting will go on as planned with almost no exceptions.

- *Ensuring attendance*—The president or CEO must ensure the priority of attendance so process owners all show up regularly. Since all of the players report to this person or are within his or her organizational hierarchy, it should not be a problem to make process owners understand the priority ranking of this meeting. It is not uncommon, early in the process, to see salespeople try to use "customers" as an excuse to miss the meeting. If the president believes that these situations can be managed by effective people, and states same, this conflict usually is not a reoccurring issue.

- *Facilitating a consistent agenda*—The president monitors and facilitates a consistent agenda. Often this is done by the administrative assistant to the president. See Chapter 6 for full details on the agenda elements.

1. Prepares financial spreadsheets.
2. Assesses business plan performance.
3. Provides trends.
4. Defines gaps in performance.
5. Drives actions from root-cause analysis.
6. Updates financial plan.
7. Ensures promises are kept to outside stakeholders.

Figure 8.4 The role of the CFO in S&OP.

- *Holding accountability*—Accountability only happens when questions are focused on understanding root cause. The president is the one who can best ask the tough questions as metric performance and actions are presented for each plan (financial plan accuracy, demand forecast accuracy, operations plan accuracy, inventory plan accuracy).

- *Ensuring documentation of follow-up actions*—The office of the president is normally where the minutes from the S&OP are documented and distributed. If a good accounting of the agreements and assignments from the meeting is maintained, better discipline can be associated with the process and, accordingly, progress gained.

Vice President of Finance/CFO (See Figure 8.4)

The financial conscience of the organization, the CFO has a very specific role to play in the S&OP process. Since the real reason businesses exist is to make a profit, the financial aspects of this process are vital. Here are some of the more typical duties and roles of the CFO:

- *Preparing financial spreadsheets*—The CFO typically prepares the financial spreadsheets for the S&OP. To be effective, these data must be documented in the same product families and groupings in which the demand and operations plans are measured. In many organizations a single spreadsheet shows all of the measures. The spreadsheet can be several pages long, as it documents the entire 12-month rolling required S&OP process horizon.

• *Assessing business plan performance*—The CFO presents performance percentage numbers for the financial plan accuracy. These performance indicators are stated by product family and include each family's accuracy in the past 30-day period.

• *Sharing trends*—It is also helpful to understand trends from month to month. Doing so gives top management a better idea of process predictability over longer periods. Because of this, the CFO should share trends showing product family financial plan accuracy, month to month, for (usually) at least the last six months. This can be very helpful in the risk management decisions that often have to be made at the S&OP review.

• *Showing gaps*—The CFO is responsible to show the delta between the plan of record and the last product family financial forecasts as communicated by the latest S&OP forecasts (forecasts are as follows: ship plan on MTO from production and the demand forecast for MTS product from sales).

• *Presenting actions from root-cause analysis*—It is the job of the CFO to present actions required to close any accuracy gaps on the financials.

• *Updating and sharing new financial plan*—The CFO also updates and shares product family financial plans going forward in the 30-60-90-day window, as well as over the balance of the 12-month rolling plan. He or she is also helpful in understanding the impact of possible risk factors in future plans through the 12-month rolling horizon.

• *Making and assessing promises to stakeholders*—The CFO normally is responsible for the promises made to outside stakeholders. When forecast changes affect these promises, the changes should

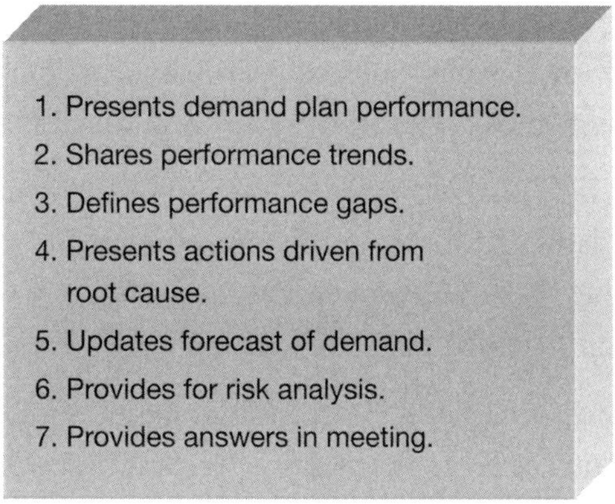

1. Presents demand plan performance.
2. Shares performance trends.
3. Defines performance gaps.
4. Presents actions driven from root cause.
5. Updates forecast of demand.
6. Provides for risk analysis.
7. Provides answers in meeting.

Figure 8.5 The role of the vice president of sales/marketing in S&OP.

be highlighted in the S&OP to make sure the CEO, and, when applicable, the board of directors, know the impact to these important stakeholders.

Vice President of Sales and/or Marketing (See Figure 8.5)

Few will argue with the importance of the role of the demand-side process owner. He or she is the communicator of the new forecast information for demand, the lifeblood of sustainability and growth. Following are the major tasks of this role:

- *Presenting demand plan performance*—The demand-side process owner presents the metric percentage performance numbers for the demand plan accuracy, by product family and for the past 30 days, to the top-management team for review.

- *Showing trends*—The demand-side top manager shows the trends of the product family demand plan accuracy, month to month, for at least the last six months. This helps to establish accuracy predictability by product family.

- *Showing gaps*—Next, the VP of sales and or marketing shows the delta between the prior demand plan of record and the latest product family forecasts.

- *Presenting actions*—Actions follow the gap analysis as lessons are learned from the past forecast performance. This top manager then presents the actions to close any accuracy gaps.

- *Updating and sharing new forecast*—The demand-side process owner updates and shares product family demand plans going forward in the 30-60-90-day window, as well as over the balance of the 12-month rolling plan.

- *Presenting risk analysis*—He or she highlights any changes affecting forecasts such as promotions, large shows, phaseouts, new product introductions, and so on, and also points out any weakness in the plan representing risks to volume, either high or low.

- *Answering questions regarding accuracy*—He or she answers any questions in the meeting concerning the forecast accuracy.

Vice President of Operations (See Figure 8.6)

The VP of operations carries the ball for the supply side of the manufacturing business. This is where the buck stops in terms of capacity, supply chain quality and efficiency, schedule accuracy, and customer service in most manufacturing organizations. These people can make or break the S&OP process effectiveness by the quality of the work they put into their risk assessment and management systems within their organization.

Here are some typical duties of the VP of operations:

- *Presenting percentage performance measures*—The VP of operations presents metric percentage performance numbers for the operations plan accuracy, by product family, for the past 30 days. This sharing helps all to understand the predictability of the operation and schedules.

- *Showing performance trends*—The VP of operations is expected to show performance trends operations plan accuracy for each product family, month to month, for at least the last six months. This is typically done on a spreadsheet and is simply an exercise of capturing history.

1. Provides performance reporting for operations.
2. Shares performance trends.
3. Provides gap analysis.
4. Drives actions from root-cause analysis.
5. Provide updates to the operations plan.
6. Provides risk assessment within operations.
7. Provides answers on operations issues at meeting.

Figure 8.6 The role of the VP of operations in S&OP.

- *Showing gaps in performance*—The supply-side process owner shows the delta between the plan of record for the last month and the last product family operations month ending actual performance. This identifies the gap between plan and actual and allows for the analysis to happen.

- *Presenting actions from root cause*—At the S&OP meeting, the VP of operations presents any actions planned or started to close accuracy gaps anticipated in the future. These are the lessons-learned opportunities from the gap analysis in performance.

- *Updating and sharing plans going forward*—The next duty of the supply-side process owner is to update and share product family operations plans going forward in the 30-60-90-day window, as well as over the balance of the 12-month rolling plan.

- *Presenting risk assessment within operations*—The VP of operations then must highlight any changes that could affect plans such as supplier risks, production shifts from one facility to another, new product introductions, and/or any other unusual circumstances.

- *Answering questions*—The VP of operations (not the master scheduler, as I see in many organizations without the right level of accountability) answers the questions in the meeting concerning the operations plan accuracy. Others in the meeting can certainly support the answers; however, it is generally beneficial if the president, asking the questions, directs these questions directly to the VP of operations. This ensures the proper accountability and knowledge going into the S&OP process and makes sure that top management is plugged in at the right detail level. Obviously, in large companies this can vary, as job descriptions vary a bit. For example, in a very large company there may be a GM that asks the questions in the S&OP meeting, and the operations manager may be the process owner in that particular division. Because it is not feasible to describe every possible organization chart, some discretion is to be used in interpreting this role item.

Master Scheduler (See Figure 8.7)

One of the most powerful and exciting jobs in manufacturing, the position of master scheduler in high-performance organizations is like being the director of an orchestra. If the relationships are managed well within the organization, the master scheduler can have great influence on both the company and the effectiveness of the S&OP process.

Following are some typical duties:

- *Preparing spreadsheets*—The master scheduler normally prepares the demand and operations plan spreadsheets with plans, including actual and performance metric performance, by product family. This becomes the centerpiece of the S&OP meeting. In some organizations even the financial information is prepared by the master scheduler through standard equations plugged into the spreadsheet. In other companies, the CFO hands off his or her data to the master scheduler or prepares separate documents using the same product family breakdowns.

- *Distributing information*—The master scheduler distributes the demand and operations plan spreadsheet to the S&OP participants

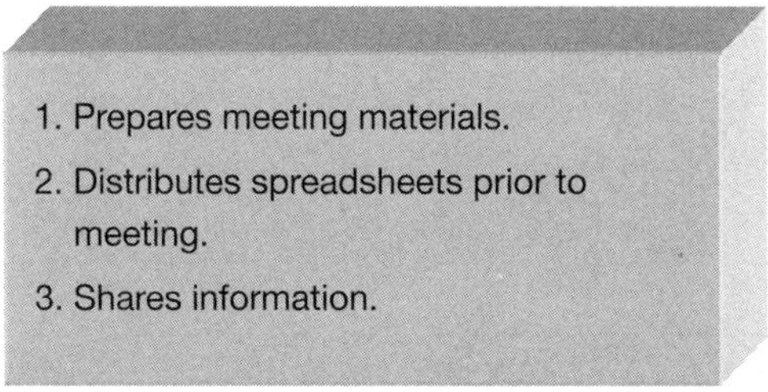

1. Prepares meeting materials.
2. Distributes spreadsheets prior to meeting.
3. Shares information.

Figure 8.7 The role of the master scheduler in S&OP.

prior to the meeting (as far in advance as possible). The minimum is at least a couple days. This gives the players time to understand their variation and make plans for adjustments. Keep in mind that there should be no surprises for these other process owners. If they have done their job, these owners will have monitored the process results throughout the month. These S&OP data are simply a confirmation that things went as they knew they did, bad or good.

- *Sharing information*—This particular master scheduler duty is a sensitive one that requires a mature organization that understands the benefits of this step. The master scheduler has knowledge of detail risk opportunities that others in the business may not have. This might include first-hand knowledge of supplier misses that have not yet shown up as real trouble or new products being behind because of, for instance, tooling design difficulties. The master scheduler in high-performance organizations is involved with many aspects of the business. Even the best CEOs cannot be that involved in the day-to-day activities. For that reason, the master scheduler should meet with the CEO/president prior to the S&OP meeting to make sure he or she knows all of the issues and can ask all of the right questions on upcoming issues. Since normally the VP of operations reports directly to the president, business etiquette comes into play, and in some organizations, the list of "concerns" is simply written down and distributed to the whole team prior to the meeting. This list then becomes a review list in the meeting. Either way is acceptable. What is not acceptable is for

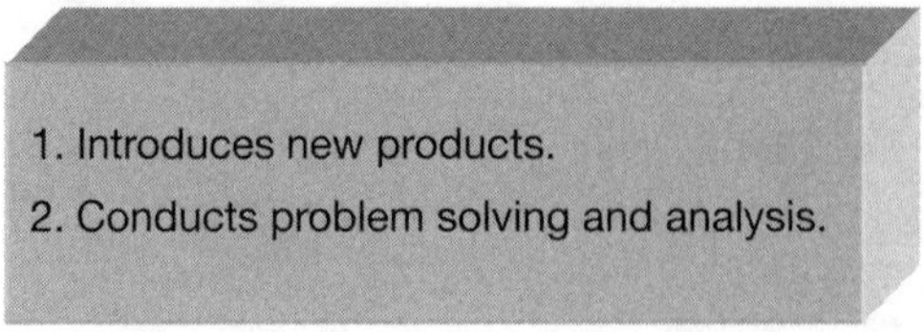

1. Introduces new products.
2. Conducts problem solving and analysis.

Figure 8.8 The role of the VP of engineering in S&OP.

the master scheduler to fail to acknowledge risks that he or she knows are not getting the proper attention. These are often the surprises that bite hard and cost the business dearly in the end.

- *Clarifying roles*—The master scheduler is not at the S&OP meeting to answer operations questions, although the master scheduler can be of assistance to both the operations and demand plan process owners in the meeting by providing data and facts.

Vice President of Engineering (See Figure 8.8)

The VP of engineering is a valuable attendee of the S&OP process meeting. This process owner of designs is usually valuable in understanding the priority and risks associated with upcoming new product introductions as well as longer-term risk opportunities. Any and all of these risks should be discussed for clarity within the top-management team.

Following are the tasks associated with this role:

- *Introducing new products*—New product introduction is typically one of the biggest risk management opportunities in the planning horizon. Engineering obviously has a big role in its successful plan accuracy. Knowledge should be shared and discussed.

- *Solving problems*—By nature, the engineering group has problem-solving skills that can often be applied to risk opportunities to minimize the possibility of process variation. This help can come in many forms. While all in the meeting have this responsibility, the engineering managers can be especially helpful with their resources.

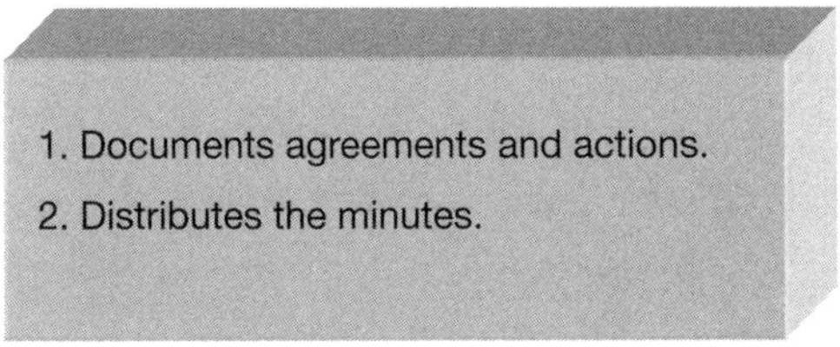

1. Documents agreements and actions.
2. Distributes the minutes.

Figure 8.9 The role of the president's administrative assistant in S&OP.

Other Possible Attendees' S&OP Meeting Duties

There are numerous other possibilities within organizations. Although including them all in a book like this is impossible, the following list may help sort out some of the possibilities that might exist and help define the expected roles within the S&OP process review.

President's Administrative Assistant (See Figure 8.9)

The president's office carries a lot of clout. Normally the assistant to the president is very efficient at listening and taking notes. This makes this person a very good candidate for taking notes at the S&OP process. There are many agreements and handshakes that typically happen at each meeting. These good intentions are best if carried out as intended. The assistant to the president can help the organization be effective.

Following are tasks associated with this position:

* *Documenting agreements and actions*—The president's assistant can be very helpful by taking notes during the meeting, including any assignments or agreements for actions.

* *Distributing the actions*—The president's assistant can aid the process also by distributing these notes in a timely manner after the meeting. This normally includes a predistribution review by the president.

Demand Manager (See Figure 8.10)

Some organizations have a demand manager. This person typically gathers and massages information needed to assemble the demand plan. He or she

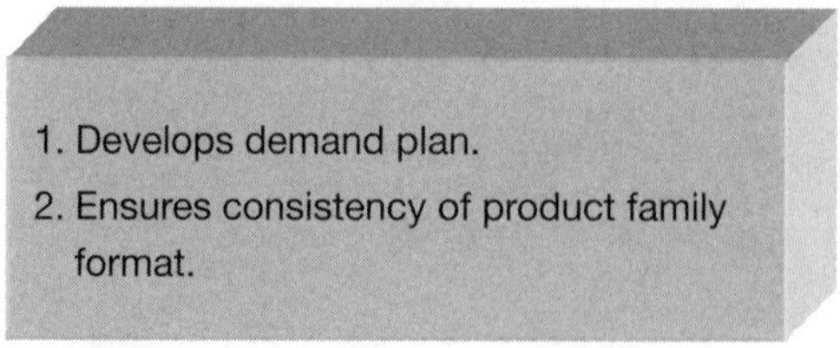

1. Develops demand plan.
2. Ensures consistency of product family format.

Figure 8.10 The role of the demand manager in S&OP.

normally works closely with the master scheduler on a daily basis and with the demand-side process owner for the monthly demand plan development.

Following are some typical responsibilities:

- *Developing and preparing demand plan*—The demand manager prepares the demand spreadsheet for inclusion in the overall S&OP spreadsheet put together by the master scheduler.

- *Ensuring consistency of demand-side data format*—The demand manager ensures that the demand and operations spreadsheets are in the same format and are in complete synchronization. This is especially important in terms of product family groupings.

- *Providing demand-side data*—The demand manager often provides facts and data to the master scheduler with regard to the demand plan risks in future plans.

Product Managers (See Figure 8.11)

Product managers typically own a product in terms of monitoring and influencing costs, margins, marketing plans, and new product development. This position is normally very influential. To leave them out of the S&OP would be a mistake. In some larger organizations, these people are the demand-side process owners by product family.

Following are some typical responsibilities:

- *Providing forecasts*—The product managers often are the ones responsible for providing forecasts for their specific product families. A demand manager of clerical support may still consolidate

1. Develops forecasts.
2. Perform marketing analysis and action plans.
3. Perform gap analysis on performance.
4. Maintain process ownership for the demand plan accuracy.

Figure 8.11 The role of product managers in S&OP.

the various product family forecasts into one document. These forecasts become the plan of record for the S&OP review.

• *Presenting marketing analysis and action plans*—The product manager usually has the responsibility of presenting actions affecting customer behavior during the S&OP. This would be appropriate if actual demand were not tracking to anticipated and forecasted demand, which would warrant analysis and explanation. Often the product manager is called upon to provide that analysis.

• *Providing gap analysis*—As the demand-side process owners, the product managers answer any questions regarding plan accuracy of their product families at the S&OP review.

• *Sharing process ownership for the demand plan accuracy*—In many organizations the product managers share full accountability with the VP of sales/marketing for plan accuracy. These product managers normally report to the demand side of the organization, often directly to the vice-president level.

WHEN IS THE PLANT MANAGER THE LEADING ROLE IN THE S&OP?

In large multifacility companies, the S&OP can be done on several levels. Plants may be established with demand specific to the facility. Many times this can be a defining factor for developing the dividing lines between product families. In these organizations the S&OP will happen at the plant level, with the plant manager and the appropriate product manager getting the hand-shake even before this data stream is fed to top management for the final-level S&OP. In these applications, the product family used at the top-level S&OP may be divided into smaller product families for the plant-level S&OP, making the process almost exactly the same as the top-level application, except that it is conducted for one plant rather than for the whole company.

If this seems confusing, it shouldn't be. Any single plant in a big company is the same as a small company when viewed alone. In the top-level S&OP in a multiplant environment, the plants are no different than departments in a smaller company. The only difference is the scale. At some point the "departments" in smaller companies become "plants" in a bigger world and qualify for their own S&OP process.

THE ROLE OF THE PROJECT MANAGER IN THE DEVELOPMENT OF THE S&OP INITIALLY

Organizations that have not started an S&OP process often designate a project manager for the role of developing the S&OP in order to start the process with the right ownership and discipline. But what exactly is the role of this project manager in the S&OP? The better this is defined, the less likely the person will end up feeling like an extra thumb (handy but not really a net gain).

The project manager is the conscience of the team in terms of good practice. When the S&OP process begins, this project manager often leads the meeting, making sure the agenda is followed and that players are disciplined about attendance and having their prework completed. Mike Steiger, the manager responsible for SIOP (as it is called there) implementation at Freudenberg-NOK, an auto-manufacturing supplier headquartered in Detroit, did exactly that as the process was rolled out in his organization. Mike would also make sure that the meetings were scheduled 12 months in advance and that reschedules were not done—or at least not easily done. His focus was to keep the team on the right track with habits and expectations. The meetings always happen on time, and the attendance is typically stellar. This makes the meeting effectiveness happen faster, bringing benefits to the bottom line.

1. Educates top management.
2. Educates the core team.
3. Provides materials for critical mass education.
4. Defines the S&OP model.
5. Coaches the process going forward.
6. Provides examples.
7. Provides network opportunities with other companies.

Figure 8.12 The role of an outside consultant in S&OP.

THE ROLE OF AN OUTSIDE CONSULTANT IN IMPLEMENTING AN S&OP PROCESS

The world of consulting is made up of all types and approaches. The approaches vary from "do it for you" to "don't really do anything." The best results normally come from something in between. When outside help is hired to completely design and implement solutions, often the result is lack of inside ownership of the solutions. Lack of inside ownership is a recipe for failure. There are some parts of the S&OP, however, that best utilize outside experts. These not only include areas not deliverable from insiders but also allow a specific model to be implemented with fewer egos and arguments getting in the way. After all, top management is involved in this process. The areas best done by outside experts include the following (see Figure 8.12):

- *Educating top management*—Outside experts, people who have been through S&OP implementations before, normally have battle scars that increase wisdom on the topic. The reason many implementations fail is almost always due to top-management issues. Outside experts that have the respect of management can point out the required role of management and even the shortcomings of existing process without the same stigma that an internal resource might find. It is also extremely important to have the top-management team and the workforce on the same page.

• *Educating the core team*—The core team ultimately is responsible for the success of the S&OP implementation. Knowing about pitfalls before they are experienced is an asset. Education from outside experts with experience from several implementations and applications in varied organizations can be a big help. These experts can provide insight into specific activities that lead to quicker results. This is a good use of outside help.

• *Providing materials for critical-mass education*—Materials can come from many sources: outside experts, APICS (American Production and Inventory Control Society), local user groups, colleges, and so on. Digital video materials are available from a limited number of sources for detailed self-facilitated education. Developing these materials internally would take months and would not be to the level of quality already available on the market.

• *Defining the S&OP model*—There are lots of variations on the theme out there. Most are different versions of the same process. Reinventing this can often be risky. It is better to start out with a proven methodology than to have to backtrack later as mistakes are realized. The entire team needs to also share the same glossary of terms. Terms are easily debated. The options are to debate the terms one at a time or to choose an outside expert that prescribes a specific version and adopt that version. (You could also use the definitions provided in the glossary of this book.)

• *Coaching the process going forward*—Outside experts can help coach both up and down the organization. My first consulting experience in this area was as a practitioner hiring a consultant for this purpose. It is often difficult for an insider to point out opportunities for top management to act differently. Doing so is much easier for a respected outsider. In fact, this is a natural role for outside experts. Top management will listen to them even when the inside information tells the same story. This is a sad but true reality, one that most are probably already aware of.

- *Providing examples*—Outside experts have examples of previous implementations. This can save time and effort.

- *Providing network opportunities with other companies in the same situation*—Being able to contact other companies that have been through this before can be helpful. This can also happen via contacts through APICS and networking at meetings, conferences, and seminars.

THE TEAM ROLE

The success of the S&OP implementation depends on the seriousness of top management and the understanding of the benefits and payback. The best training in the world supported with the best process design will not get off the ground without top-management dedication and attention to the process details. In the best organizations, S&OP is actually driven from top management. They expect good process and put process owners in place to deliver those results. The team has the job of carrying through on actions and agreements made in the meeting. Follow-up on all actions should be tracked through meeting minutes and reviewed each meeting. Implementation and the role of the team in that application are covered later in the book.

✻ ✻ ✻ ✻

9

CONNECTING SUPPLIERS TO THE S&OP PROCESS

Suppliers are obviously the lifeline of any manufacturing company. If the supplier's process links directly to the customer's, the opportunity for lean and flexible results exists. In some companies the objective is not just cheapest cost from suppliers, but instead lowest cost through the supply chain. This requires commitment to the cause of process linkage and handshakes on common goals. These goals can include flexible lead times within certain product families, inventory buffered in strategic points to offset process variation, and differing cost points depending on forecast information and accuracy. In the mid-1990s, AlliedSignal (pre-Honeywell) Transportation and Power Systems actually paid for training for its suppliers so that these suppliers could gain from learning techniques for executing a robust S&OP process. They were a pretty successful team under the direction of Bill Amelio at the time. Some of that success certainly was due to the commitment to the S&OP process and making sure they and their suppliers were on the same page every day of the week. Today, many companies are starting to understand that the goodness seen from an internal S&OP can be multiplied if extended into the supply chain network. It just makes sense and is the next natural step in lean evolution.

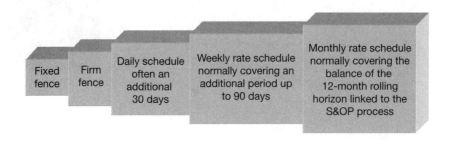

Figure 9.1 Typical supplier time fence agreements.

WHAT WOULD BE SHARED WITH THE SUPPLY CHAIN?

Usually suppliers are limited in the number of product families with which they are involved with a customer, although that is not necessarily always true. Whatever product families they are specifically supplying are the families that need to be shared. The product family information includes short-term daily need, mid-term weekly requirements out 60 to 120 days, and monthly buckets in the 4- to 12-month range. These product family forecasted requirements should correspond with the time fence agreements with the supplier. See Figure 9.1.

For each of these fences, rules of engagement should be agreed upon. These rules might include schedule flexibility expectations, lead time expectations, and even premium charges for changes. Of course, all of these agreements depend totally on the market conditions and leverage of each player in the supply chain. Anytime partnership arrangements can be agreed to that reduce surprises, the result is a positive. Supply chain management has received a lot of attention in books and seminars in the last few years—with good reason. Whenever performance is anything but synchronized with the procurement schedule, costs are incurred. To many businesses, managing the supply chain means reactionary expediting and priority freight. High-performance businesses do not work that way. Good supply chain management means that the critical suppliers share information daily, per shift, or even more frequently (hourly). Whenever changes are made to the schedule, suppliers are involved in the decisions, especially when lead times or rules of engagement are violated.

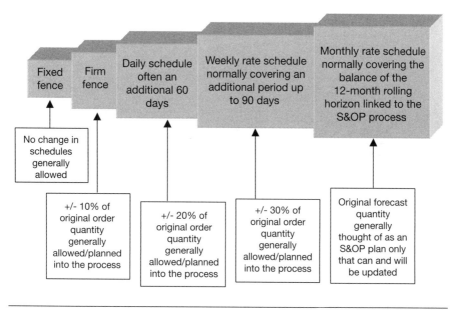

Figure 9.2 Time fence norms and flexibility built into the planning horizon.

Figure 9.1 demonstrated typical time fence agreements. Figure 9.2 adds the flexibility handshakes that can be very helpful. Keep in mind that the percentages are for discussion purposes only and can vary from business to business. These agreements depend on many aspects, including cost and investment requirements and stability in the market.

In a high-performance organization, within the "fixed fence," there should be little schedule movement. Any changes to the schedule within this short time frame need to be cleared with the supplier. Remember that this time frame does not have to be very long. Table 9.1 shows results of an unscientific survey on average time frames for the fixed fence.

Most businesses are tightening their fixed fences to shorter periods, at least compared to just a few years ago when "frozen schedules" were often quoted (but seldom actually firmly executed) at two-week levels. This means that suppliers are often forced by market conditions to determine inventory strategies (MTS, MTO, etc.) to meet these requirements. All of this plays toward a robust S&OP process for efficiency of process. Understanding the inventory strategy of critical suppliers is very helpful in understanding risks in the S&OP discussions and decision making.

Table 9.1 Fixed Fence Time Frames

Time Frames	Percentage	Cumulative Percentage
1 day	35%	
2 days	25%	60% within 2 days
3 days	5%	65% within 3 days
5 days	20%	85% within 5 days
2 weeks	10%	95% within 2 weeks
Over 2 weeks	5%	

If 60 percent of manufacturing firms have schedules with their customers that are only fixed for about 48 hours, some thinking has to go into being ready for changes in the 49th hour. Not many businesses have the luxury of full cumulative lead times of less than 48 hours. That requires inventory strategies that buffer inventory somewhere in the supply stream. Accordingly, if there is a 30 percent flexibility requirement in the second month, suppliers will not be as surprised if the S&OP process yields a major change in that time frame. Sharing the S&OP each month as changes are made and giving the suppliers an understanding that the top-management team is blessing these numbers gives them some assurance and actually allows these suppliers to incorporate this information into their S&OP process as well. The agreements for change and flexibility are referred to as the "rules of engagement" in many businesses. This is exactly the same topic as the rules shared with internal demand- and supply-side teams that are represented at the monthly S&OP meeting. Figure 9.3 adds one more step and indicates sample time frames for the fences and points out the rules of engagement.

In the figure, flexibility is part of a handshake at the beginning of the relationship. In this example, for a particular product family, the supplier knows exactly what the requirements are for flexibility of schedule. This way there are fewer surprises. The agreed-to rules of engagement are clear. If the supplier in this example has a cumulative lead time of 24 days, inventory strategy comes into play immediately. Table 9.2 clarifies this handshake.

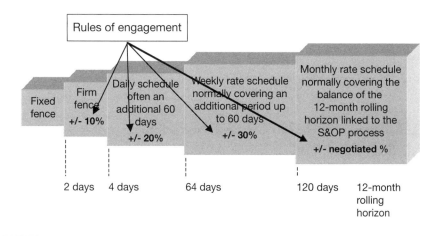

Figure 9.3   Time fence norms and flexibility built into the planning horizon.

WHY DEVELOP PARTNERSHIPS WITH SUPPLIERS?

Lean thinking has taught us in recent years that costs eliminated anywhere in the supply chain are good for *everybody* in it. Partnerships are special working relationships that allow and foster sharing of technology, forecasts, and financial information. "Partnership" in this context does not refer to the legal term and does not suggest any special legal implications, although they are not excluded from the process. Partnership in this context could be as simple as sharing information and linking the S&OP processes of the two organizations for mutual benefit. When members within the supply chain trust each other and work closely, there is great opportunity for the elimination of waste and duplication of effort. Clear rules of engagement allow for better, more robust

Table 9.2 Flexibility Requirements Table

Time Frame	Schedule	Lower Limit	Upper Limit
0–2 days	100 per day	100 per day	100 per day
3–4 days	100 per day	88 per day	112 per day
5–64 days	100 per day	80 per day	120 per day
65–119 days	100 per day	70 per day	130 per day
120–365 days	100 per day	no limits	no limits

planning within an organization. The S&OP process is where many of the schedule changes are made. By having shared well-understood and recognized rules, there is a much less likelihood of bad decisions regarding lead time violations, heavy expediting costs, and/or missed schedules.

SELECTING SUPPLIERS FOR PARTNERSHIPS AND S&OP SHARING

When judging supplier performance, most materials managers will instinctively answer "quality" when asked what the most important measurement for supplier value is. It is a conditioned response. Just about everyone has "read the book." In high-performance organizations, delivery from suppliers is almost as high a priority as quality. Price is a distant third in those manufacturers.

Continuous improvement, on the other hand, is not as often regarded with the same fervor. Yet, in most cases, continuous improvement is as good a sign as any for supplier value. Knowing that a supplier is constantly after yet another notch in quality, responsiveness, or cost reduction gives most customers a feeling of confidence and the supplier a reputation for reliability.

Most companies that set out to link their S&OP process with the supply chain do not partner with every supplier. That would not make sense. Instead, some suppliers are simply given the outputs of their S&OP, *details* for the current and near-term plans, and rate for the broader-scope planning horizon. Since there is some time investment for robust S&OP linkage among companies, the decisions should not be taken lightly. Here are some criteria for selecting a potential supplier for a closer partnership relationship:

1. *Criticality*—When a company is considering partnerships with suppliers, it must consider criticality. Some suppliers are easy picks because sharing technology, financial information, and forecasts seems to come naturally. In some cases, the mutual benefit of sharing information is not as obvious, and in others, sharing too much information is risky for competitive reasons. Often in more commodity-type markets, the best suppliers supply both you and the competition. This makes for strange bedfellows.

When S&OP information is shared, the risks run higher of competition getting the run rates and new product information plans in the future—not something that is normally considered good. Before the S&OP linkage is introduced in its entirety, this should be taken into consideration.

2. *Reliability*—Before a company considers a supplier for any partnership agreement, reliability needs to be both examined and experienced. Being able to rely on a supplier and be confident that the supplier will deliver when and what you need is a huge asset. Reliability comes in many forms. Here are some areas to think about in this regard:

   • *Quality*—Reliability of quality processes and product is minimum table stakes in today's competitive markets. Without reliability, suppliers should not even be on the "approved" list. Quality of process is defined by having repeatable processes, management systems to ensure compliance, and metrics in place to warn of process variation as it develops. Most high-performance organizations measure FTQ (first-time quality) to pick up any issues or opportunities in this space. FTQ is a good indicator of quality process.

   • *Integrity of promises*—Reliability is only meaningful if it includes reliability of promises. Promises in this category include dates met on new product design commitments for components, quality improvements, cost reductions, and not least important, delivery of product to the customer's door. Along with this comes the trust that when problems arise (and they can, even in high-performance organizations), there will be an early-warning system to allow plan realignment with minimal loss. A company that is reliable prior to an S&OP linkage effort should be able to reduce costs within the supply chain once information and understanding are shared in detail. It may seem like the company has to be perfect prior to inviting it to share in the S&OP link, but in fact, it is the "good" companies that offer the best opportunity to put

good planning information to use. Sharing with poor companies can also help performance, but one might easily wonder
why a poor supplier is a supplier of choice anyway!

- *Responsiveness to schedule changes*—Suppliers are not usually
the only reason for schedule changes with a customer. More
often customers cause the process variation. Remember that
the list of requirements discussed in this section apply to not
only suppliers but every company. Everybody is a supplier. It is
your responsiveness to customer need that requires equal or
better responsiveness from your suppliers. The further down
the food chain, the more responsive the parties need to be.

3. *Competence*—Just as with reliability, competence has many faces.
There is no reasoning behind developing partnerships with suppliers that lack trustworthy competence. Being reliable is good;
being reliably competent is great. There are a few expectations in
this area:

- *Technical expertise*—If a company makes the highest-quality
goods, it should also understand the technology behind these
products. Only a few years ago most businesses could afford
full R&D (research and development) staffs. With the competitive markets today and lean thinking, most companies are
relying on suppliers for technical assistance in their field of
expertise. This only makes sense. Total cost is incurred
throughout the supply chain, not just in your factory. If you
have engineers designing the components that are purchased
and later assembled, there will undoubtedly be some duplication of resource sitting at the supplier's site. Often the easiest
component-design-related resource to eliminate is yours. The
real core competency is in the design of the final product,
using component technology. Obviously, this is not always the
right answer, but it often can be. Once suppliers take on this
responsibility, it becomes all the more valuable to have a fully
linked S&OP process connecting the two businesses as seam-
lessly as possible.

- *Financial stability*—Supplier profitability has not always been at the top of priority lists with customers. It is not generally the focus of everyday concern. Customers who have experienced a bankruptcy of a single-source critical component supplier usually end up thinking differently. Financial stability is the enabler to allow design improvements, capacity investments, and risk taking for the sake of improvement. Linkage with suppliers through the S&OP gives more visibility to these issues.

- *Improvement history and plans*—With competence comes the willingness and tenacity to stay at the head of the pack. All great companies have a continuous improvement track and measure progress and results regularly. Some progress is visible to the customer, but not all of it. The S&OP also gives visibility to these improvements as capacity and flexibility grow. A partnership handshake with a supplier should provide evidence of internal process improvements.

4. *Location*—This topic is controversial at best. I have had several clients in the United States that have recently sourced offshore. NAFTA (North American Free Trade Agreement) was some of the influence, but China's favored-nation status with the United States has also been a major driver. Probably some would keep this topic off the list of qualifiers for determining potential partnerships. There are no hard-and-fast rules about the importance of supplier location. There are always trade-offs. Distance equals cost, and adding either is bad. Unfortunately, many top managers today look closed-mindedly at offshore sourcing and ignore the real costs. This thinking creates pressure through the chain of command that allows logic to sometimes be set aside. This is not to say there are no good offshore sourcing decisions made. However, there is a need for more thought and consideration than has typically been applied to this topic.

    Location is on this list not because there are recommendations that always apply. It is on the list because the risks are many and the rewards are not always as significant as planned. Human beings know some processes well, and yet not others. Supply chain managers are good at getting components across great distances (thanks to rail and ships) at relatively low cost. They are also good (thanks to priority freight companies) at getting components across great distances quickly. But they are not good at getting components across great distances quickly *and* cheaply. The "and cheaply" part of freight transportation is not always baked into the planning initially, and sometimes bad decisions are made.

There is another way to look at location as a competitive advantage. One client I work with is a blow molder engaged in lower-volume packaging needs, mostly for the food and drug industry. Opposite from the offshore approach, their strategy is to build plants across the street from their customers. In the past few years they have built two new plants and are getting ready to break ground again. This strategy has created and funded their growth.

Many organizations that are moving offshore for components are staring to require buffer within a radius of the customer's facility. This, of course, comes at a price also. Again, there are always trade-offs. If and when these types of decisions are made for critical components, the S&OP shared information could be very helpful in bringing to light problems before they occur.

5. *Price*—Notice that price is last on the list. This does not mean it is not important—after all, it is on the list. Price is a very important element, just not as important as reliability and competence. The three-legged stool (purposely leaving location out of it) would be pretty wobbly without any one of the legs. (See Figure 9.4.) Price does not always need to be the lowest. Price needs to provide good value. Very few high-performance companies have made their success on price only. Most of the best companies in terms of growth and stakeholder return are not the lowest priced

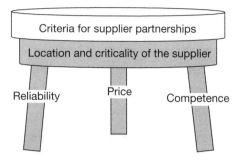

Figure 9.4 Three-legged partnership criteria stool.

in their markets. The common denominator is value. Value is built from product quality, service behind the product, and people behind the products and services.

The S&OP process brings to light changing prices and, accordingly, updates to margins for the customer. It is often helpful for offshore suppliers to, at least, share their S&OP 12-month rolling horizon of anticipated price/revenue.

IMPLEMENTING SUPPLIER S&OP PARTNERSHIPS

Once suppliers are chosen for partnership development, the next question to answer is how to go about successful implementation. Project management is a proven process, and each supplier partnership implementation should have a separate project, with a team leading, measuring, and supporting the progress.

Following are the tasks involved in implementing partnerships with suppliers:

1. *Define the scope of the project*—Like any project, the first step is to define the scope. When does the group get to celebrate victory? How long do they have to accomplish this? What are the deliverables from this partnership in terms of information sharing in the S&OP?

2. *Choose the team*—The team and team skills and knowledge are obviously very important. It cannot be exclusively lower-level individuals, although there is good reason to have people from within each company that understand the details of how the information systems work. Following are the members in a typical partnership implementation team:

- *Sponsor* — Customer VP of operations
  (or VP of procurement if there is one)

- *Team leader* — Customer purchasing manager

- *Team members* — Customer materials manager

  Customer planner for this product family

  Supplier account manager or salesperson

  Supplier master scheduler

  Supplier product manager for this product family

- *Support personnel* — Customer IT (information technology) manager

  Supplier IT manager

3. *Develop the implementation plan*—The implementation plan is no different than any project. The elements of the plan should include the following tasks:

- Collect data that describe the current "as is" condition. How do the S&OP processes currently run and what do the spreadsheets contain?

- Define the expectations in measurable terms—the "should be" state. How could the information be best used and in what format would it best be communicated?

- Develop plans to close the gap. Define each step, who is responsible, who process owners are once the S&OP linkage is established, and what the metrics are. The metrics should be the same as those used in this book to describe proper S&OP metrics.

- Process-map the information flow, product flow, and technology or knowledge flow that happen both today and in the future model. Show how information will be reviewed prior to publication and when and how the sharing of information will happen.

4. *Create and assign actions in Gantt chart format*—Document all the expectations. Do not lose original promise dates even when rescheduled. Maintain two columns, original and revised dates. Following are additional tips:

- Drive actions to move the relationship to the desired state where goals are shared and metrics are compared.

- Measure the results and adjust as necessary.

- Document the policies and rules of engagement.

- Monitor results of the policy execution. This takes special attention because there is not total control over suppliers, especially if the partnership is one for convenience and not legally binding. Because of the nature of information sharing, many companies choose to have nondisclosure agreements signed in advance of the S&OP linkage.

5. *Celebrate*—Too many teams forget to celebrate success. This does not require fireworks, but if the desired outcomes were met, some recognition is in order. The celebration spotlight helps educate others in both organizations on what good behavior looks like. It is not just about the team members, but also the rest of the organization. There will be lots of additional partnership agreements to implement.

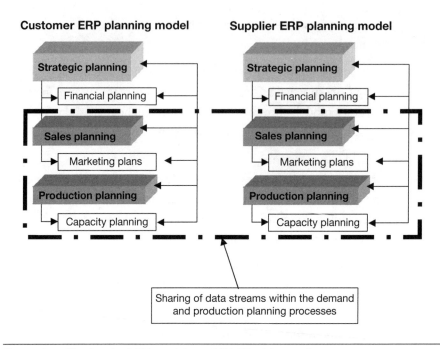

Figure 9.5 Aligning the ERP models and S&OP with suppliers.

ALIGNING THE S&OP PROCESSES

The most rewarding effort in terms of information flow is the alignment of the S&OP processes from one business to the other. Figure 9.5 illustrates the alignment using the ERP business model as the schematic.

The information streams coming from the S&OP processes are the most up-to-date information available and also the more reliable and accurate. It is never perfect because the information is a prediction, but it is the best available. It should be shared. Depending on the size of the product family and impact of the supplier, in some organizations the suppliers actually attend the S&OP meeting for their particular product family. In most, however, the information is forwarded as soon as the meeting is adjourned and plans are blessed.

INFORMATION SHARING

There are many types of data that businesses within a food chain can share profitably. The possibilities are endless, but here are a few ideas:

- Demand plans

- Production/operations plans

- Pricing information on shared commodities (negotiate on things like steel or resin)

- New product introduction schedules and expectations

- Quality control techniques

- Changeover improvement techniques and expertise

- 5-S techniques of workplace organization and housekeeping (The 5-S technique was developed years ago in the Toyota corporation and has been written about extensively in lean manufacturing texts.)

- Continuous improvement techniques

- Measures

- Technical information on products manufactured

- Competitive analysis

- Strategic goals as they relate to shared interests

- Business imperatives as they relate to shared interests

Depending on the specifics, the information sharing can go well beyond this list of obvious topics. Sometimes companies will share other nonproduct-related information, just to help the supplier be as professional as possible. This might include things like safety practices, Six Sigma training, lean training, Class A management systems and methodologies, and human resource policies. There are few limits in this space when it makes sense to be as closely linked as possible.

Table 9.3 Supplier Certification with S&OP Element

Rating Category	Weight	Rating System
Quality	30%	95% sustained = Certified supplier
• Perfect orders		90% sustained = Qualified supplier
• Packaging quality		80% sustained = Approved supplier
• Count accuracy		
Delivery	40%	
• Promises always met		
• Flexibility in schedules		
Value-add services	30%	
• Short lead time		
• Technical support		
• Consigned inventory		
• Other value-add processes		
o S&OP process in place		
o Demand and operations plans go out 12 rolling months		
o Sharing of information is current and dynamic (not static)		

SUPPLIER PERFORMANCE RATINGS AND CERTIFICATION

Supplier rating and certification is typically a strategic tool in quality and cost improvement. The S&OP process lends itself to be included in this rating system. Metering supplier effectiveness is best done with three elements: quality, delivery, and service. The objective is to keep subjectivity out of the equation as much as possible, realizing supplier ratings will not be completely nonsubjective. Table 9.3 is a traditional approach to supplier certification with an added element of S&OP process requirements.

The application of this model normally includes written criteria for each level within the topics of quality, delivery, and value-add services. This can be developed in conjunction with the supplier or independently. It is always best to have the supplier review the criteria prior to implementation. If small adjustments are necessary, the ownership in the end product will be improved.

Supplier Status			Characteristics
Certified Supplier a) Minimum of three perfect receipts b) No rejected material for six months c) Quality, delivery 95% d) Value-add services 95% e) Audits optional	**Qualified Supplier** a) No rejected material for six months b) Quality, delivery 95% c) Monthly performance review d) S&OP plans shared e) Annual audits	**Approved Supplier** a) Last receipt perfect b) No rejected material for three months c) Quality 95% d) Delivery 90% e) S&OP processes attended by both for both organizations f) Audit every six months	

Figure 9.6 Maturity profile specifics.

Classes on proper S&OP process execution can be very helpful, as can letting the supplier sit in on your monthly meeting for a couple cycles. In a little more advanced model, Figure 9.6 shows the maturity model of supplier relationships, including the S&OP linkage.

Within the supplier rating system there is normally a maturity profile that rates progress of the supplier base. There is some leeway in these ratings, as evidenced by many high-performance organizations. Figure 9.6 gives some suggested categories and rating criteria for a supplier maturity profile.

CAUTION REQUIRED

There will be times when a supplier is "the only game in town" and criteria are not met for full approval as a supplier. The partnership is a forced relationship. Sometimes because of business need, the choice to jettison the supplier is not an option. This is not a favorable position to be in, but it is not terribly unusual. The mission objective is to get out of this position as soon as possible. The options are not always apparent, but some that should be considered include coaching an alternative favored supplier into adding the additional product line, looking out of the area for an alternative supplier, adding the capability to your own facility, or coaching the existing supplier to improve. Shared metrics can be powerful in this regard. There is no magic potion here, but the lesson has been learned by many organizations over the years. Do not accept poor suppliers any longer than absolutely necessary. This is an easy thing to say and not always easy to do, but it must become a business imperative when in this vulnerable position.

A FEW WORDS ABOUT THE INTEGRATION OF LEAN AND SIX SIGMA PRINCIPLES IN PROCUREMENT

As with most high-performance ERP topics of discussion, the integration of lean and Six Sigma principles is a no-brainer. True high-performance ERP cannot be sustained without this type of thinking.

- *Lean*—The elimination of waste is enjoyed quickly within supply chain management as lead times are reduced. Every time a day is struck from the lead time of a widely used product, the associated inventory for that 24 hours is eliminated as well. Using the technical resources of suppliers instead of funding them in-house is another example of the lean principles being utilized. Each time the quality is improved and process variation from suppliers is reduced, lean principles are engaged. Without lean thinking, efficient supply chain management cannot exist.

- *Six Sigma*—Project management has lots of opportunity within the supply chain management space as well. Improving quality, eliminating inventory, implementing supplier partnerships, coaching setup reduction at the supplier site—these are all examples of project possibilities. When Black Belts—that is, people who have high project management and problem-solving skills—are engaged for the accomplishment of these tasks, the supply chain gets a little more effective.

PROCESS OWNERSHIP

The procurement manager is the natural process owner for the S&OP procurement process and for supply chain management. In some larger organizations there might be a VP of procurement. Duties of this process owner include tracking metrics, reporting performance, performing root cause analysis of process variation, driving change through actions, communicating the performance to the suppliers, following up on audits and supplier assessments, managing supplier partnerships, and tracking practice to the current policy. This is no small task and one that is left to strong-willed, skillful leaders in high-performance organizations.

CLASS A ERP OR HIGH-PERFORMANCE ERP METRICS IN PROCUREMENT

The metrics in Class A ERP procurement focus on system linkage and synchronization. Although supplier metrics seem to be a significant part of supply chain management, the metric emphasis in Class A is bigger than just looking at the supplier. The real opportunities in Class A come from making sure that the business system is maintained to the latest MPS and that the suppliers are absolutely in line with the latest schedules. When the master scheduler changes something in the MPS, unless the suppliers are hardwired to the revisions, little gain will be seen from making the change in the MPS. For that reason, the procurement process metric in Class A is the percent of complete orders that are received on the day that they were required. The S&OP process, although not as specific, can aid in this understanding as well.

WHAT METRICS WOULD MAKE SENSE IN THIS INFORMATION CHAIN?

There are some generally accepted measures in the ERP space that fit well into an open relationship between customer and supplier. When the S&OP is being linked, many times there is a much more open relationship, allowing these enhancements. Some of the more valuable measures for suppliers (from the customer perspective) are the traditional Class A ERP metrics:

- Monthly

  - *Operations plan accuracy*—Ability to predict by product family how many units will be produced in the month.

- Weekly

  - *MPS accuracy*—Percent of orders that are completed with full quantity in the week they were scheduled.

  - *Materials planning metric*—Percent of orders let with the full lead time (according to the item master in their system).

- Daily

  - *Inventory accuracy*—Percent of location balances that match perfectly to their system perpetual location balance.

  - *Bill of material accuracy*—Percent of bills of material that are perfect (three-way match: 1. specification, 2. ERP system, and 3. what is done on the production floor).

  - *Daily schedule adherence accuracy*—Percent of orders that are completed (full quantity) in the day they are scheduled.

  - *Shipping performance*—Percent of complete orders that ship on the day of the original promise. Some companies have taken this from daily to hourly (percent that ship on the originally promised hour).

Many times these weekly and daily metric results are shared once a week between the partners, with the monthly measures shared once a month. Since the S&OP process is a discussion about performance, it works well to incorporate these measures in the shared S&OP information. It creates a good baseline for performance understanding beyond the S&OP metrics.

HOW DO COMPANIES INITIATE THIS SUPPLY CHAIN INFORMATION LINKAGE?

Obviously the relationship has to be good before a partnership linkage can be established. Usually it is the customer that initiates this relationship, but in some rare instances, the supplier can influence the customer to create the S&OP linkage between the two companies. If the company in question meets the criteria of critical supplier, has reasonably good process currently, is stable and reliable, and does not supply major competitors, it is generally a good candidate. The best way to initiate this linkage is to invite the supplier's top management to a monthly S&OP meeting. Let them see the value in the process and help them understand the need if costs are to be optimized. Hopefully there would already be a high degree of trust, but if there are any issues in this regard, have them sign a nondisclosure prior to the meeting so that free-flowing discussion can happen.

OUTCOMES FROM SUPPLY CHAIN S&OP LINKAGE

When a supplier/customer S&OP partnership linkage is established, the results are very obvious. Immediately the supplier has full visibility into the customer's future needs and also has some understanding of the focus and expectations. Communication is not simply between the buyer of one company and the sales team from the other. In this new scenario, top management of both organizations regularly share information monthly, giving both advantages within risk management.

WHICH SUPPLIERS DO YOU CHOOSE?

The suppliers to partner with are the ones that you need the most and are most suited to aid in the development of your business. This includes technical capability, quality awareness, continuous improvement desires, and financial stability. Start with the ones with the biggest impact to your business and

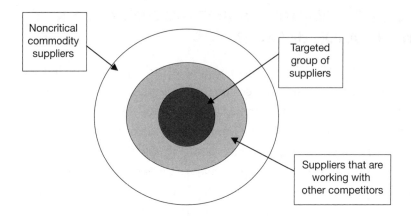

Figure 9.7 Targeted suppliers for partnership.

keep working down the list until you have partnered with all of the key suppliers. This generally is not more than 25 percent of the suppliers. Another 25
percent are general suppliers and could be supplying the competition as well
as your business, and the delta are generally commodity suppliers and not
critical. See Figure 9.7.

* * * *

10

GETTING IT RIGHT: EVALUATING RISKS AND METRICS USED

Metrics are one of the most important drivers within the S&OP process. Top-management planning processes that do not put the proper amount of attention on the measures often miss one of the biggest opportunities to drive excellence. The metrics are the dashboard indicators for efficiency, learning, and effectiveness. In the case of the S&OP process, the metrics are few but critical. They are business planning accuracy, demand planning accuracy, and operations accuracy. Additionally, metrics like deliver on time or data accuracy are often solid indicators of performance and can be made visible without taking a lot of additional time from the meeting.

MAKE SURE THE METRICS ARE VISIBLE

When the S&OP meeting first gets off the ground in an organization, often the use of measures to drive activity is a new concept. If this is the case, it is important not only to focus on the performance metrics but also to link them to the required actions. For example, when the meeting starts, the first agenda item is typically the financial performance, or business planning measure. If, for example, the performance is in the 90 percent range, many might feel that the performance is adequate, especially if the actual percentage number is not discussed. If, for example, the discussion drifted away from the percentage and focused on other factors only, different conclusions could be reached. Here is a possible scenario:

- The performance for customer service is good and no customers are complaining enough to be heard at the top-management level.

- The business for most of the product families is steady (not growing or declining).

- One product family is declining in sales and it is not well understood why.

- The overall financial performance is reasonably close to goal, but the declining family is offset by one family that is selling at a more profitable mix.

The situation as described may not generate much concern if the performance measures by product family are not discussed properly. In this case, one might get the feeling that financial performance is acceptable, especially if the percentage numbers are not a focus. Now change this same scenario by only the way it is looked at by the top-management team:

- Customer service to the original promise is reported at 92 percent. Difference in scenarios—92 percent is unacceptable.

- Of the five product families measured, all except one are at 95 percent financial plan accuracy.

- The one family that is out of line is also the family that is declining. The performance measure for the business plan accuracy for this renegade product family is 65 percent. Now the discussion takes a completely different perspective. By visibly showing and focusing on the accuracy measures and keeping a minimum acceptable level high enough, management attention goes right to where it can influence the business the most: in areas of risk and concern.

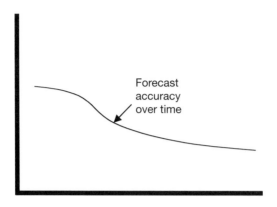

Figure 10.1 Accuracy of forecasts over the planning horizon.

- The overall performance, while important, is only a reflection of what is going on at the product family level. If each gets the right attention, much more predictability will result.

If the culture in top management is focused on the performance minimums with an obligation to ratchet these goals when met, the likelihood of obtaining real performance gains is much higher. Don't confuse this with bad management. Even top managers, when the metrics are not at the right level of granularity, can miss the performance risks until they are obvious. The best time to catch the opportunities is before they reach that point. Bottom-line, high-performance management teams will not rely totally on "gut feel" and financial plan measurements only. By reviewing measures and understanding the drivers for process variation, much of the risk connected with new product introductions, new suppliers, new customers, and/or new markets can be minimized.

HISTORY BEFORE THE 12-MONTH HORIZON FORECAST ACCURACY

Even though never perfectly accurate, the 12-month horizon is valuable. Statistics show that the 30-day horizon is normally the most accurate part of the plan and plan integrity decreases as the horizon increases. See Figure 10.1.

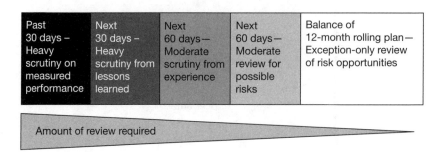

| Past 30 days – Heavy scrutiny on measured performance | Next 30 days – Heavy scrutiny from lessons learned | Next 60 days— Moderate scrutiny from experience | Next 60 days— Moderate review for possible risks | Balance of 12-month rolling plan— Exception-only review of risk opportunities |

Amount of review required

Figure 10.2 Review scrutiny.

REVIEW SCRUTINY

Because of the criticality of the short-term plans, the scrutiny needs to be the highest in the shorter horizon. High-performance management planning processes create accountability for current performance. This requires the first and maybe the most important review to be on the last 30 days past. This is the review on the short-term forecast that 30 days ago was the 30-day outlook. By looking at this recent past performance, a company can learn many lessons that apply to the near future. These include lessons on customer relationship management, supplier capacity risks, market movements, and so on. See Figure 10.2.

Other metrics that come into play in this review are the measures of normal performance of both the demand and supply sides of the business. These measures are not necessarily a component of the formal review but are often visible at the meeting in case the performance measurements warrant further understanding. Having these measurements ready can shorten the investigations and increase the understanding quickly. Some common shared measures *beyond* the required S&OP measures might include the following:

Demand Side

- *Market share by product family*—Percent of gain or loss within certain markets associated with each product family.

- *Customer retention*—Percent of return customers. This measure may not be available each month. In some companies this is a quarterly measure.

- *New customers added*—Percent of new customers within the last quarter.

- *Sales funnel*—Number of possible orders or projects or line items, not closed, in the sales pipeline.

- *Sales cycle time*—Time from first acknowledgment of possible sale to close of order.

Supply Side

- *Efficiency*—Earned hours of cost standard compared to available hours.

- *Uptime*—Percentage of available hours that the plant was fully running.

- *Scrap*—Dollar value of materials and labor scrapped. This should include materials even when salvaged, such as "regrind" in plastics companies.

- *First-time quality (FTQ)*—The percent of units completed in operations not requiring tweaking or unusual adjusting to meet specifications during operations.

- *Out-of-box quality (OBQ)*—The percent of units that are perfect as delivered to the customer.

- *Customer service*—Percent of complete orders that are shipped on the original promise or, as ratcheted, the percentage of complete orders received at the customer's site on the requested date.

- *Data accuracy*—Percent of inventory balance accuracy, BOM (bill of material) accuracy, accuracy of standards, routing record or bill of resource accuracy, etc.

Of course, each company will vary slightly on the necessary measures. When metrics become a regular component of the S&OP and are always available, top managers can, at will, bring the data into the discussion as discrepancies in the normal required S&OP measures—business plan, demand plan, and operations plan—are reviewed. It can be very helpful on many fronts.

WHO PREPARES THIS EXTRA DATA?

Organizations vary in structure, but most often the master scheduler is a key player in assembling the data and spreadsheets for the S&OP process. This would include assembling or packaging measurement data even though the process owners of the measures are a much more likely source for capturing this measurement data. The master scheduler is a key resource in most high-performance organizations, both in large and small companies. With primary involvement in all of the manufacturing schedules, new product introduction, customer priority decisions, supplier capacity constraints, and other risk opportunities within the supply-side operation, the master scheduler is often one of the most knowledgeable sources for getting up-to-date information on 12-month horizon and where the risks may lie. In this position of awareness, the master scheduler, if carrying the proper amount of responsibility, can provide extremely valuable insight on process risk and pending variation in the planning process. This is exactly what the S&OP process is in place to accomplish.

This is not to take any emphasis off the value of top management's direct involvement; without it, this process does not add value, nor is it effective. Instead, with the *additional* value-add from the master scheduler, top management can have the best chance of being tasked with the decisions from all of the high risks, ones they are already aware of and a few that may only be visible from the eye of the production floor. Obviously there is a much higher likelihood of production floor awareness within top-management ranks in smaller companies. The real opportunity is not who brings this extra awareness into the meeting, but only that is gets there.

EXTRA METRICS AND RISK OBSERVATIONS IN THE NORMAL S&OP PROCESS

The agenda should be consistent and stable in the S&OP process. Extra risk opportunity information brought into the light of this important management system simply brings full value to the process. Top management, especially the CEO or president, is the agenda referee on decisions concerning what gets discussed, how far the discussion is taken, and what gets dismissed or delegated offline. Think of this extra information as other key indicators that might affect decisions regarding the normal discussions on business, demand, and operations planning. The agenda is maintained with the last 30 days of performance, next current forecasted expectations, and longer-term visibility in all three of the top-management 12-month rolling plans.

If the top manager wants to add elements to the review not dictated by the templates in this book, let it be. If the topics link to the existing S&OP agenda, the process can actually become more powerful. At The Raymond Corporation in the 1990s, Ross Colquhoun, then CEO, liked to have the marketing plans reviewed at the monthly S&OP meeting. Product managers were expected to address actions they were doing to affect customer behavior. Because this top manager was totally engaged in these actions and had strong opinions as well as market knowledge, he insisted that as the forecast was presented and evaluated, the accuracy was reviewed. This agenda worked perfectly.

Another CEO at a packaging company insists that capacity charts be reviewed at each S&OP for all of the machine lines. In this company these equipment investments are substantial and, if fully utilized, represent the best opportunity for ROI (return on investment). The past few percentages of machine utilization represent low-cost, highly profitable work, and top management wants visibility to this open factory capacity. Again, this fits nicely into the agenda.

Probably the real message here is the need to stick to the base agenda— review the percentages on performance for the last 30 days and then look carefully at the rest of the horizon with scrutiny on the next 30 days, moving out to an exception-only focus at the 9- to12-month component of the horizon. If the top-management team desires more detail, experience shows that if the appetite is there for it, it will only add value to an already proven process.

* * * *

11

CONNECTING THE S&OP PROCESS TO CUSTOMERS

For obvious reasons, customers are much more difficult to manage than are suppliers. The linkage between the S&OP processes, in good supply chain management, is no less valuable, however. There are no secret weapons aimed at getting the right level of influence over customers. Each situation is a little different, and each organization needs to establish relationships, given the opportunity. However, to know the end result is to have the right objectives in mind as the journey begins. The S&OP process, if fully integrated with the customer's S&OP review, gives way to much improved service as well as lower costs by limiting the risks of low inventory and creating shared goals and actions. In this chapter some desirable outcomes of shared process are outlined (see Figure 11.1).

Shared Process Examples

1. Marketing plans are shared to allow preparation for anticipated increases in sales. This could be any of a million possibilities.

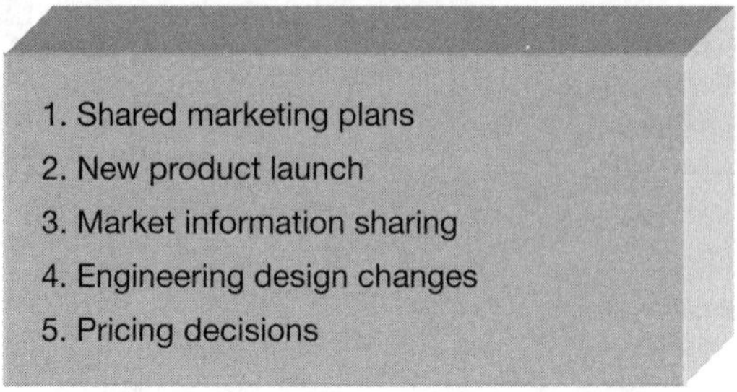

1. Shared marketing plans
2. New product launch
3. Market information sharing
4. Engineering design changes
5. Pricing decisions

Figure 11.1 Drivers for sharing information with your customers.

Following are just a few:

a. *The customer is planning a coupon program in a large regional advertisement*—This is always information that is good for supplying organizations to have. It allows better control of inventory levels to support service requirements increasing.

b. *The customer is planning to attend and populate an advertising booth at an important show that is expected to spike demand*—If the show is successful, more demand will be created. Knowing this is important in the supplier planning process, for material and capacity.

c. *The customer is releasing a large new ad campaign*—Like the coupon impact, new ad campaigns can affect demand in a major way. Being ready for this is a great asset.

2. New product launch. Following is a possible scenario:

a. *The customer plans to phase out an old product in about nine months*—As a supplier, phaseouts are not always known without the information sharing from the customer. This information allows the reduction of component inventory synchronized with the customer's plan, reducing cost and inventory exposure.

b. *The customer decides to offer specials at the point of a new product introduction to convert their market to the new configuration*—Customer specials can impact demand for new products in ways not anticipated. Information is welcomed at this level and often does not get shared completely enough. The S&OP process creates the correct environment for this sharing.

    c. *Demand signals within the customer's market are dramatically changing mix*—Any information from the market is especially helpful. For example, a bottle molder serving several markets such as pharmaceutical, sauces and syrups, shampoos and cosmetics, and dry snacks does not understand every market served with the same expertise that their customer who works specifically in that market does. By partnering with their customer in each market, they get a much more informed view. This allows them to tool properly and plan capacity for the anticipated demand shifts.

3. Information sharing regarding customer's market, such as the following scenarios:

    a. *Technologies driving change at the customer's market can affect demand both up and down*—Engineers at the customer are the right people to tap into to understand where technology is taking their market. While not always perfectly accurate, they still are valuable to partner with.

    b. *Changes in mix expected through the customer's forecast*—Each company has a unique view on its market that is not always as clear from one level down in the supply chain. The S&OP process is done by product family and therefore gives good insight into the customer's mix change expectations.

    c. *Obsolescence of some components*—With the mix change comes the obsolescence of some components. Any sharing of this information ahead of time can save increases in scrap at the end of the product life.

4. Engineering and design changes. Following are just a few possibilities:

   a. *Break-through technology that will change the market as soon as the new product is launched can be quite secretly handled prior to announcement*—New technology can impact markets and does every day. Some of this is not easy to detect before it happens, but the more information and discussion that happens each month about this risk, the more opportunity there will be to improve the risk situation. Nondisclosure agreements can eliminate risks in this area and allow full sharing of information.

   b. *Customer beliefs that the market will be changed by new products being launched*—As new and improved products are introduced to the market, the mix of demand often changes. The S&OP information discussed each month by product family can give important insight.

   c. *Phaseout of some models*—Sometimes customers, for one reason or another, will phase out certain models. The more headlights that are shone on this prior to the actual phaseout, the better the coordination can be managed.

5. Pricing decisions such as the following:

   a. *Raising prices can be a strategy to discourage demand in some older models*—Like other market-shifting forces, price is a major influence in any market.

   b. *Raising prices to move the market to a different mix*—Again, good information is invaluable for reducing risk.

   c. *Lowering price to increase demand*—Just as price increases can discourage certain demand, decreases can have the opposite effect, causing panic in the supply chain if not understood and forecasted ahead of time.

   d. *Lowering price to liquidate inventory in discontinued models*—Liquidation means ending the cycle of demand. Increases in demand due to a liquidation strategy can catch suppliers off guard with extra inventory made because of these increases. Understanding the background is very helpful and can change the supply chain actions dramatically.

There are as many ways to document the opportunities for information sharing as there are companies to share it. Getting your customers to share this information by letting you, the supplier, participate in their S&OP is not always easy. The discussions in this meeting are understandably very sensitive. At the very least the resulting output information needs to be shared.

Some customers don't even have an S&OP process. This makes it especially difficult! Many companies have taught suppliers the benefits of the S&OP process. Companies with a strong, solid relationship with their customers may improve this relationship even more by teaching their customers the steps in the profitable review process called S&OP.

* * * *

12

THE S&OP PROCESS IN SERVICE INDUSTRIES

Every company has a common belief at the start of the conversation on process change. It is usually stated like this: "You do not understand; our business is different." Even a good friend of mine, who works in government agency social services, used that statement the other day. The reality is not as clear, however. In fact, there are many commonalities from business to business—many more than differences at this level. Service businesses, from a standpoint of S&OP, are not very different at all from manufacturing firms. If you substitute the word "service" each time product or units are described in the normal S&OP process, the descriptions generally work as stated.

TYPES OF SERVICE ORGANIZATIONS AND APPLICABILITY TO THE S&OP PROCESS

Several different applications of S&OP are described in this section. It should become obvious that this process will work in just about any business and create value. The following lists are not complete but are instead a sampling of various businesses to give a better, more clear idea of the possible application of the S&OP process. Hopefully the variation is enough to give a sense of the application of S&OP. It would take too many pages to name all of the potential applications.

1. *Engineering services groups*—In the mid-1990s AlliedSignal's Transportation and Power Systems Group (now Honeywell) set out to apply the Class A ERP model to its engineering services group. The S&OP process was, of course, at the top of their business model. The company quite effectively planned capacity and demand of its product families in a monthly S&OP review very similar to the review held in its manufacturing operations that included the demand team. AlliedSignal's product families were variations on design, testing, and documentation. The review included measures on the company's customer service of delivering these services as promised to the division. It was initiated as a result of gains in manufacturing at the company through Class A ERP focus and the belief that engineering could generate similar gains. These insightful managers were proven correct.

2. *A major investment firm* has used the Class A ERP process and S&OP to increase its effectiveness in the marketplace. This stock brokerage firm buys and sells equities for its clients. The S&OP process allows the firm to review expectations monthly. Just as in any operation, capacity is important to plan for, and forecasting is a helpful process tool.

3. *Many major store chains* use the S&OP process to estimate future demand and, accordingly, inventory requirements. This is especially important at the Christmas season, with increases in demand.

4. *In freight hauling*, the S&OP process becomes very valuable to predict capacity and demand. Product families might include package size and geographic demand. Again, this can be especially helpful in holiday seasons, where more demand is required.

5. *Warehouse businesses* can gain from the S&OP by predicting and assessing risks for space requirements and manpower planning.

Levels of temporary employees can be planned as well, with actions starting well ahead of the actual demand increases.

6. *Colleges* can use a similar process to predict demand from marketing efforts and anticipated student fallout. This helps these organizations keep the right amount of students in-house and helps keep the teaching staff relatively stable.

7. *Consulting companies* use this process to evaluate resource requirements and financial health. The consulting company I started my consulting career with in the 1990s used a monthly S&OP review process, and DHSheldon & Associates LLC continues the tradition.

8. *Banks*—Demand for money and services makes the banking industry perfect for an S&OP process review. Each month the 12-month rolling plans should be reviewed for capacity and financial impact. By looking at these plans by product family monthly (such as mortgages, CDs, checking, business loans, etc.) and reviewing the risks, companies can take actions in time to adjust for anticipated changes in demand.

9. *Social services*—Predictions and plans to keep services in alignment with demand can be helpful when hiring, budgeting, and delivering services such as heat assistance, food stamps, and medical assistance.

10. *House painting service*—A house painting company can benefit greatly from the planning of resources and demand. This is true of both single-person firms as well as larger multiworker organizations.

11. *Phone companies*—Like every other service or manufacturing business, resources have to be planned. Hurricane season could even be planned as a risk factor in the 12-month rolling plan, causing extra demand for trucks and manpower to repair downed lines. Product families might include things like repairs, installs, load for telephone capacity, and so on.

12. *Manufacturing suppliers that only procure products*—Many organizations supplying manufacturing supply chains do not actually manufacture product. Instead, they procure products from various sources and kit them or offer them at an increased price with shortened lead time and higher delivery fidelity over alternate sources. These organizations generally offer inventory as a service, and by evaluating risk, the possibilities of obsolescence and excessive inventory are reduced. These companies benefit from a robust S&OP process. An O-ring supplier in Minnesota buys most of its products from Asia. By using a robust S&OP process, the company is able to minimize inventory and cost risks.

13. *Doctor's offices*—We all know that doctor's offices could benefit from capacity planning linked to a forecast and measures showing customer service to these forecasts. It helps eliminate the waiting we have all come to know at many offices. Not enough doctors have gotten the message!

Hopefully at this point it is becoming clearer that there are virtually no businesses that cannot benefit from a healthy S&OP process owned and led by the top management of the firm. If demand forecasts are created and accuracy is measured, lessons are learned monthly from the review process. While not perfect, these forecasts offer insight into the ability or lack of ability to foresee the demand for the business. Even when demand is not predictable, if this fact is acknowledged and reviewed, more emphasis can be brought to bear on that topic and buffers can be devised to lessen the impact to service and profits of the company.

A service is simply a product that comes without a box. Many companies recognize this fact and develop robust plans that consider demand risks. These companies survive and prosper, with more predictability. There is no reason not to be enthusiastically involved in an S&OP process regardless of the type of business.

THE DIFFERENCE IN A SERVICE ORGANIZATION

The differences might be small, but there are just a few differences in application in a service organization:

1. *Units of measure* within a product family would often be non-product such as hours, dollars, people served, and days billed.

2. *Demand and capacity can be spread out* over a large geographical area and not in one manufacturing facility, as is often the case in manufacturing. This often impacts the product family design.

3. *Profitability* is handled differently in nonprofit service organizations. Budgets, however, are still important, requiring financial health to be linked to the S&OP just as in any manufacturing organization.

Service organizations are more similar to manufacturing firms than different when it comes to the application of the S&OP process.

* * * *

13

IMPLEMENTING THE S&OP PROCESS

This chapter covers a proven methodology for the successful implementation of a robust S&OP process. Keep in mind that top-management ownership is a prerequisite to this success regardless of implementation techniques. If top management is not engaged, implementation will be extremely difficult and maybe impossible if management cannot be converted. Few things in life are that sure.

STEPS FOR SUCCESSFUL IMPLEMENTATION

Following are imperatives for the implementation of S&OP:

1. Education of all parties

2. Establishment of goals and vision

3. Organization structure for change

4. Measurements and data collection

5. Accountability and management systems

6. Documentation

7. Training for sustainability

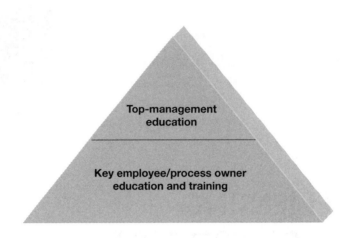

Figure 13.1 Layers of education and training.

Let's look at each of these in turn.

Education of All Parties

To get everyone on the same track right from the beginning, there needs to be shared goals, a common glossary of terms, and a shared vision. This is best done through education. Don't think of this as teaching "old dogs new tricks," as the saying goes. Think instead of this as reorganizing thoughts we have all had before into a central and shared focus. It is sort of like light shining through a magnifying glass. When the whole team is on the same path, change can happen quickly. This is the goal—make it happen as quickly as possible while keeping the spirit of the goal clearly in front of the team.

Initial top-management education (see Figure 13.1) usually takes about four to six hours and is normally done in one sitting. In this session there will be a lot of emphasis on top management's role for successful implementation. This includes the S&OP process roles, management system roles, and "walking the talk." It typically is done by outside experts simply because top-management people do not always listen well to insider direction. Also, by getting this education done early, top management can easily position themselves as the champions of this process implementation, a powerful signal to send to the organization.

Education of the rest of the team comes in waves. The second educational focus will come with the core team. The core team is made up of process owners from the major processes (business, demand, and operations) within each facility or plant. Each plant will have its own core team headed by the top manager for that plant. Education in these teams can be done in several ways. The most effective way for the company is to have this education delivered by professionals that can not only explain the basics but can also give examples of their experiences with other companies. This can be especially effective in the early stages as converts to and advocates of the S&OP methodology are won over. Content on this core training should include detail education on topics matching the processes in the Class A ERP business model (see Figure 13.2) that feed or get output from the S&OP process.

Initial ERP education, usually a full day in duration, covers the entire gamut of ERP, but follow-up education for the more detailed courses is best done in smaller increments and can take weeks to finish. APICS courses, outsiders, and purchased video can all play a part in this important information transfer.

All people in the company will eventually be introduced to the concepts of ERP. Some of this training is delivered most effectively by the managers of the people being trained. This approach puts special emphasis on the management team understanding the basics of ERP, as well as sends the strong message that this is important and not just another float in the parade, one that "might miss me if I stay quiet and ignore it." Again, purchased video education can be very helpful in this regard by using managers for facilitators, although outside education, again, can offer an especially effective alternative. The earlier that video education can be introduced, the more cost-effective the delivery can be. This, of course, also depends on the commitment to quality facilitation.

Establishment of Goals and Vision

An S&OP start-up normally takes three cycles to achieve value-add process. This includes process owners showing up with their homework done, top management totally engaged, the president asking the right tough questions, and the spreadsheets done to properly show performance to plan. It is often

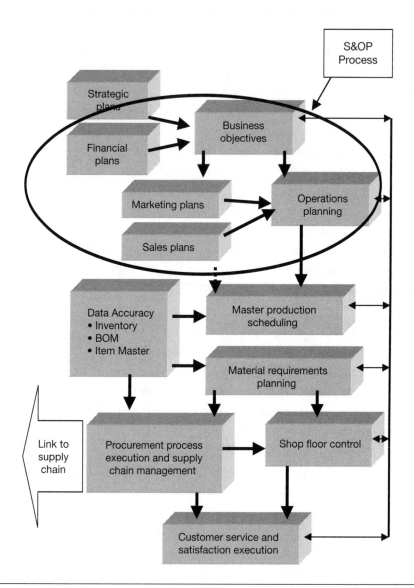

Figure 13.2 ERP business model.

valuable to have an outside expert attend these first few reviews to maximize the effectiveness in the shortest amount of time. It also can stop/avoid many of the process disagreements that can happen in this new top-management planning process. The goal of this meeting should be the following:

1. *Month one*—Education completed, assignments made, and process ownership defined for all top-management plans. These need to be ready for the end of the current month and go as many months as can be forecasted. The first month to be reviewed will be the following month (month two). The product families need to also be determined. The standard rule of thumb for number of product families is to keep it at a number less than 12 families, if possible; 6 is ideal.

2. *Month two*—The first S&OP meeting is held to review the plans "locked" as the plan of record in the beginning of the preceding month. This meeting should be held early in the month, workday two to five, no later if at all possible. In this meeting the agenda should be as follows:

   • Review performance of last 30 days—business, demand, and operations plans.

   • Review next 30 days for any risks or changes to the plans (business, demand, operations).

   • Review the 60-, 90-, 120-day plans, progressively lessening the scrutiny as the horizon increases. The objective here is to look for risk in service or financial performance.

   • On an exception-only basis, review the rest of the 12-month rolling plan. If the plan does not go out the entire 12 months in this first S&OP, the assignment for the demand-side process owner is to have it completed prior to the next review cycle.

   • Document any actions discussed.

Organization Structure for Change

There are a few steps that can aid in the effectiveness of the S&OP start-up. The short list is as follows:

- *Make sure the master scheduler is up for the task.* This position requires leadership and problem-solving capability. In high-performance organizations, this position is a high-level management position usually reporting to the plant manager or VP of operations, depending on the existing structure. The job will include coaching and leading the start-up of this important process. This person must be able to communicate in the finance organization as well as within operations. Typical master schedulers can come from operations, finance, or sales.

- *Determine the process owners for the S&OP.* This is not a difficult decision. These process owners should be obvious, but nonetheless this assignment needs to be formally determined, documented, and announced. The operations plan is almost always owned by the VP of operations. The demand plan owner is from sales or marketing and is normally the VP of one or the other. In the business where I started out, the process owner for the demand planning process was the VP of marketing, but many businesses want the accountability in the sales department. There is no question that it is a shared process, but someone needs to be the owner. Both sales and marketing need to be involved intimately.

- *Develop a schedule for the S&OP meetings to be held each month—out at least 12 months into the future.* Schedule this as "the first Monday of the month" or "second workday" or some similar method.

- *Finalize the kickoff date and how it will be communicated.* It is good to let the entire materials team know and understand this new process, as they can feed it with pertinent data.

Measurements and Data Collection

The measurements needed in a Class A S&OP process are already determined. The Class A ERP model, including the S&OP metrics, has been around a long time and has been proven time and time again. That eliminates a lot of wasted time sitting around debating (arguing) about what these measures should look like or how the calculations should be done. Don't waste time implementing these metrics. Assign the process ownership and get the metrics in place—the quicker the better. Top management must take the ball and visibly show their ownership in the top-management metrics reviewed at the S&OP process meeting. A visible board needs to be hung quickly in a conspicuous place. One plant in Anderson, South Carolina, used four huge white boards to show its metrics in oversized letters and numbers in the lunchroom. There was no missing it and the commitment to keeping it up was obvious. It showed the employee base that top management was serious.

Accountability and Management Systems

In a multiplant environment, every site should have a champion responsible for the successful implementation of its part of the overall S&OP process. It is important to pick the right leaders for this implementation, and the master scheduler normally fits the bill. The typical minimum characteristics for a successful master scheduler at the site level include the following:

- Deep product and process knowledge

- Leadership characteristics

- Well respected within the organization

Documentation

Once processes are determined and discipline requirements are designed, documentation must be completed. This is the final chapter in the implementation. Doing documentation gives the organization a chance for sustainability. Once the documentation is completed for the first set of processes, auditing should begin. This is normally done by the comptroller's office, just as it would audit inventory accuracy for the asset register. ISO has a good expectation for documentation auditing, and Class A ERP process documentation should go into the ISO-controlled documentation as soon as it is written and approved.

Training for Sustainability

The documentation sets the stage for training materials required for ongoing sustained process predictability and performance. Training responsibilities need to be part of process ownership, as well as backup planning for succession and process owner backups. This includes training within the sales and operations teams to make sure that new team members are fully aware of the S&OP process and their role in feeding risk information into the data for review. This includes positions such as sales manager, materials manager, purchasing manager, and production managers.

RATCHETING THE GOALS WHEN APPROPRIATE

As the metric performance is met, the expectations need to be ratcheted up. It makes no sense to have process owners without goals for improvement. Keep the objectives realistic but continually improving in final goals and expectations. For the sake of celebration and achievement, goals generally should not be ratcheted until the existing objectives are met and are proven to be sustainable for a few weeks.

CLOSING

Class A ERP with the S&OP process at the top of the business model is a basic required step in the journey to world-class excellence. By focusing on the goal of process predictability, schedule adherence, and data accuracy, a company can gain a great deal of competitive advantage. It is not the end-all; it is just the first step. The objective of this book was to show lots of evidence that the S&OP process not only makes sense but is important to get the most from your continuous improvement efforts. Good luck on your journey to excellence and Godspeed!

* * * *

APPENDIX A: S&OP CHECK SHEET FOR EXCELLENCE

A robust S&OP process is evidenced by a few indicators. In this appendix the abbreviated short list is shared for audit purposes. The checklist is divided into three categories:

1. *Process*—This is the check on the process itself. Robust process can be repeated with reasonably predictable results. In the case of the S&OP, given the deliverables expected, the check is to make sure the process is designed to focus on the correct areas.

2. *Management systems for accountability and sustainability*— Having the right process is good. Being able to maintain that process over time is even better. High-performance organizations have management systems in place that facilitate accountability. In the case of the S&OP, it happens every month within certain parameters. The demand review is a supporting process that happens weekly in most organizations.

3. *Measurements for results and performance*—The test for robust process, ultimately, is the resulting performance. In high-performance organizations, measures are the lifeblood—a window into company health.

CHECK SHEET

Class A S&OP (Also Known as SIOP) Process

Process

- The S&OP review happens every month at a predictable time and place.

- Top management consistently participates in the process monthly.

- The top manager of the facility leads the review (CEO, president, plant manager, etc.).

- The spreadsheets are circulated to the process owners at least three days prior to the S&OP review.

- The agenda is as follows:

  - Review last 30 days performance including the performance accuracy percentage.
    - Business plan
    - Demand plan
    - Operations plan

  - Review next 30, 60, 90 days for exceptions.
    - Business plan
    - Demand plan
    - Operations plan

  - Review on exception-only basis the rest of the 12 rolling months.
    - Business plan
    - Demand plan
    - Operations plan

Management Systems

- The S&OP review process is scheduled 12 months in advance.

- The S&OP process is almost never (no more than one time a year if you need it quantified) preempted.

- Measures are administered and reviewed each month for business, demand, and operations plans.

- Top management accepts process ownership at this level.

- An agenda is followed at every review.

- The meeting is managed to time limits but does not end if the discussion or specific decisions are not complete.

- Management comes into the meeting with their homework done. This is evidenced by answers already anticipated prior to the meeting.

- Performance less than 95 percent drives lessons learned.

- A demand review is held at least once a month prior to the S&OP review. (Most organizations do this weekly.)

- Agreements and action items are documented and distributed at each meeting.

- Action items are reviewed each month from the preceding review session.

Results

- The business plan performance by product family is 95 percent accurate or better.

- The demand plan performance by product family is 90 percent accurate or better.

- The operations plan performance by product family is 95 percent accurate or better.

- Misses lead to actions.

- Performance is posted and well communicated to the rest of the organization.

* * * *

APPENDIX B:
WHEN AND HOW TO
CELEBRATE SUCCESS
IN THE S&OP PROCESS

Celebrations are part of the learning process in organizations. Think of them as just a component of the education plan. Calibrated celebrations obviously depend on the appetite of management and the willingness to show positive feedback even when the ultimate goal has not been met. There is an appropriate time for celebration. Here are some ideas about when and how high-performance organizations might celebrate success. Keep in mind that some of these are appropriately simple, small celebrations, but nonetheless, they are positive points to underline good behavior.

WHEN TO CELEBRATE

- Often the demand plan accuracy starting point can be bad. If the demand plan accuracy was much less than 80 percent in the beginning of the S&OP process implementation, when 80 percent is reached, it is a definite celebration point—not the goal, but a good progress point. Accordingly, as appropriate, celebrate at other points along the journey.

- If the S&OP starts off with difficulties of any kind, such as not all the top managers make the meeting because of schedule conflicts or not everybody has his or her measurements in order with good data, the first time these problems are corrected, a celebration is in order to support continued good behavior. In this example, it might be as simple as some positive feedback for the people who have most recently made the process complete and effective.

- When certain milestones are met in any of the measures, appropriate celebrations or acknowledgment can be helpful.

IDEAS FOR SMALL CELEBRATIONS

- Positive feedback from the top manager in front of the entire staff attending the S&OP. This can be surprisingly effective, especially if it has been rare in the past.

- Coffee and donuts brought into the meeting paid for by either the company or the top manager.

- An announcement circulated on the bulletin boards describing the progress of a certain area (business plan, demand plan, operations plan). Make sure it is well described so employees can understand the significance of the achievement.

IDEAS FOR LARGER CELEBRATIONS

- For progress such as when profitability hits the plan exactly (or beats it) for the first time in months, management might cook hot dogs and hamburgers for the entire employee base.

- Pizza could be brought in by the truckload for the employee base for significant achievements.

- One plant manager took the entire plant to a lobster dinner for significant gains in productivity.

- Another plant in South Carolina invited the local high school band to march through the plant playing. This was especially attention getting. Obviously, safety has to be a high consideration here.

- Fresh cider and donuts might be brought in for the entire workforce.

- Walnut plaques with certificates attached can be quite effective when given for the right reasons and under appropriate circumstances. An example might be effort and results for special contributions such as regional demand plan accuracy supporting the overall accuracy.

- These same individuals contributing to the accuracy of the S&OP planning process could also be given tickets to a local sporting event. (Often businesses have season seats anyway.)

- One business in Syracuse, New York, used to award performance with tickets to seminars downtown at the fancy Syracuse Hotel. This was good on many fronts.

- Open the vending machines for the day with full disclosure as to what the celebration is about.

- Fill in your own idea.

* * * *

GLOSSARY OF TERMS

ABC analysis—The stratification of inventory into levels associated with monetary and/or volume levels. Materials planning utilizes this methodology extensively in planning methodologies.

APICS—American Production and Inventory Control Society. This organization of professionals is the keeper of the body of knowledge for inventory planning topics and process flow materials. It can be reached at 800-444-APIC.

ATO—Assemble to order. An inventory strategy that master-schedules assemblies for availability when demand happens. Subassemblies and/or components are assembled after the demand signal. Dell Computer has made this strategy famous in recent years.

audit—To audit a process such as inventory accuracy is to check accuracy of a process by a defined periodic check and measure.

balance by location—An inventory balance for only one location where a material or item is stored. This should not be confused with having more than one item in a location. They do not address the same subject.

BOM—Bill of material. The BOM is a record file that documents the description of all component and ingredient relationships including "quantity per" and all item and material numbers. It normally resides in the computer business system, but copies may also be available in the engineering design systems.

BOR—Bill of resource. The BOR is a record file that documents the BOM information along with the routing records. It documents the sequence of materials used in the process by tying each component to a process step.

brainstorming—Brainstorming is a technique used to develop ideas in a problem-solving effort. Team members take turns submitting ideas, which are documented for later review.

Buker, Inc.—Buker, Inc. is a consulting organization in Chicago that is involved in ERP education and training, including video offerings (www.Buker.com).

business imperatives—Business imperatives are the shorter-term business objectives that must be done in the next 12 months for competitive advantage as determined by top management. Not to be confused with strategic objectives, which are longer term.

business system—A computer system used to communicate linkages between business processes such as scheduling and execution of schedules, inventory consumption and balance records, forecasting and planning inventory, financials and operations, and other critical process elements. Business systems are usually referred to as ERP (enterprise resource planning) systems.

Class A ERP—A specific high level of performance using ERP methodology and defined by measurements and certification criteria. There are organizations (such as DHSheldon & Associates) that certify this performance level by auditing performance. The metrics are usually around five areas: Prioritization and Management of Business Objectives (includes Project Management, Human Capital Management, and Investment and Business Imperatives), Sales and Operations Planning Processes, Scheduling Disciplines and Production Planning, Data Integrity, and Execution of Schedules and Plans.

consultants—Experts hired from outside your organization to aid in the implementation of an improvement in process. Often education and training is a good application for consultants.

cumulative lead time—Cumulative lead time is the summary of all lead time required to requisition material and convert this material into saleable inventory. Normal sequences include procurement, fabrication, subassembly, assembly, testing, and shipping.

cycle count—A cycle count program is designed to schedule and periodically audit inventory balances for accuracy. Normally it is done using random sampling with a plan to count certain segments completely over specific periods of time. There can be wide variation in cycle counting programs depending on the process control in a particular store's area.

demand planning—Top-management planning processes include demand planning. Demand planning is the process that results in the forecast of customer behavior as it relates to a business's product sales. Inputs to demand planning are normally as follows: business planning goals, marketing plans, sales cycle knowledge, customer knowledge, and history of seasonality and cyclicality.

DHSheldon & Associates—Consulting company involved with ERP education and training including inventory accuracy. Donald Sheldon is the author of this book and is president of DHSheldon & Associates.

discipline—In inventory control and manufacturing environments, discipline normally refers to the action controls required for predictability or repeatability of a process. Processes need good disciplines or controls for repeatability.

ECN—The engineering change number describes the serial number of a change as it is being made and after it is completed. This is sometimes called an ECO (engineering change order).

ECO—Engineering change order. Same as an ECN.

ECR—The engineering change request usually is the prerequisite to the ECN. This is the process and document used to suggest a change to a product. An ECR is not an authorized change.

end items—Finished goods ready to ship. This refers to products in both MTS or MTO environments.

ERP—Enterprise resource planning. A methodology of linking and measuring business processes for the objective of high performance and low cost. Emphasis is on capacity and realities of process. Evolved from the MRP II process methodology, ERP adds more emphasis on linkages outside the business (suppliers and customers). Sometimes referred to as supply chain management.

ETO—Engineer to order methodology is used in manufacturing when the demand signal has some of the necessary information to properly complete a product. The manufacturing process is not started until the customer has ordered the item, which signals engineering to spec the job.

finished goods—Finished goods inventory is inventory that is customer-ready and could be sold and delivered in the time it takes to pack and ship the product.

fishbone analysis—A method or tool for problem solving using a fishbone diagram and process. Usually the factors considered include sources of variation from the following: methods used in the process, machinery or equipment required, manpower or people factors, materials, or environmental issues.

5-why diagram—Problem-solving process for breaking bigger problems into smaller components and determining causes.

forecasting—Forecasting is the process deliverable from top-management demand planning. The forecast is designed to predict customer behavior, taking into consideration both history and actions to affect that behavior. In high-performance businesses it is updated and reviewed at least monthly, and more recently, it is often reviewed weekly.

inventory—Material, components, or finished goods held for or used in the process of manufacturing or distribution.

inventory control—Inventory control involves the process of storing, moving, and managing the inventory of an organization. Elements include managing obsolescence, excess, accuracy, availability, and general levels of inventory.

inventory record—A computer system record showing the quantity of on-hand inventory of any specific item or material.

inventory stratification—The stratification of inventory into levels associated with monetary and/or volume levels. Materials planning utilizes this methodology extensively in planning methodologies. See ABC analysis.

Ishikawa diagram—Cause-and-effect problem-solving tool using a fishbone diagram and process.

item master record—The master record by part number within the computer system where vital information linked to that item or material is kept.

JIT—Just in time. Same as lean manufacturing.

lean manufacturing—Lean manufacturing process focuses on eliminating waste or cost-added activities in all processes in the business. Objectives of lean drive flexibility and speed of process.

location—Labeled area where inventory can be or is held. The location description is also sometimes referred to as the location.

master scheduler—The master scheduler directs the development and execution of the master schedule. He or she helps direct the "rules of engagement" between the demand signal and the supply-side delivery process.

master scheduling—Master scheduling is the process of linking demand and top-management planning processes to the factories or procurement in a manufacturing or distribution business. The master schedule creates the drumbeat for the supply chain and gives specific direction on both planned and unplanned schedule requirements.

materials management—Materials management is the functional group responsible for scheduling, planning, procuring, and controlling inventory in a manufacturing organization. In some manufacturing organizations, procurement is in a separate functional group.

MPS—Master production schedule. This is the process during which all product is scheduled through a factory or distribution facility. It normally drives requirement signals into the planning process and sets the drumbeat for the future requirements.

MRP—Material requirements planning. A subprocess of ERP that nets available and scheduled inventory against requirements from the master schedule. In most companies today, this process is done in some form for materials planning in future time buckets.

MRP II—Manufacturing resource planning. The predecessor to ERP (see ERP). MRP II was a business planning system in the 1980s and 1990s that integrated capacity planning and top-management planning with materials planning and plan execution. It was changed to ERP in the 1990s with the integration of supply chain management.

MTO—Make to order. When organizations plan subcomponents prior to the customer demand signal and finish manufacturing the product after the customer order, it is referred to as a make-to-order environment. MTO is usually referred to as an inventory strategy.

MTS—Make to stock. When organizations plan and build finished-level inventory prior to the customer demand signal, it is referred to as a make-to-stock environment. MTS is usually referred to as an inventory strategy.

obsolescence—High-performance companies define the point at which inventory is no longer expected to be used in any reasonable time frame. Usually inventory that is not planned to be used in the next two years or more would be considered obsolete. This often becomes an issue when engineering change orphans a part due to a replacement design.

Oliver Wight—Consulting company involved with ERP education and training including S&OP.

Pareto chart—Frequency chart of root causes. In this case it refers to the root cause of inventory inaccuracies.

procurement—Procurement is the purchasing function within an organization responsible for procuring items required by the company. Responsibilities usually include contract negotiations, supplier selection, pricing, reverse auctions, and supplier performance.

repetitive manufacturing—Repetitive manufacturing is an environment where the same items are often repeated. System shortcuts can make sense, and many business systems are set up specifically to accommodate this type of efficiency.

routing—See routing record.

routing record—Documented description of the process steps used in manufacturing or converting raw material and/or components into finished and semifinished goods.

strategic objectives—The strategic objectives are longer-term goals for an organization. These goals tend to define the priorities and outline of top-management expectations going forward. The time frames are usually in the two- to five-year range.

stratification—See inventory stratification.

tolerance—Generally acceptable inventory accuracy tolerances. For inventory, balances are A = ±0 percent; B = ±2 percent; C = ±3 to 5 percent. These tolerances are allowed for less expensive parts for efficiency. Many manufacturing operations do not use tolerances.

24-hour rule—When inventory is stored in an area (by process design or normal habit) for more than 24 hours, it falls into the 24-hour rule. In this situation it is generally considered responsible to know where this inventory is by tracking it in the business system. Inventory that is held less than 24 hours in any one area often is tracked at the next 24-hour point or at finished goods.

work order—A work order is used in some businesses to define a specific job requirement with configuration requirements and quantity required. In a repetitive environment, work orders are often not used.

* * * *

INDEX